CONTENTS

Level 11

UNIT 1: SCENES OF WONDER

UNIT 2: WORLDS OF CHANGE

UNIT 3: WINNING ATTITUDES

UNIT 4: GETTING TO KNOW YOU

UNIT 5: TAKE THE HIGH ROAD

Grandma Essie's Covered Wagon

Klondike Fever

My Adventures at the Center Of The Earth

The Silent Lobby

UNIT 6: ZOOM IN!

Sentences

Read the paragraphs. At the end of each sentence, write the correct end punctuation (period, question mark, or exclamation mark).

Do you know how much of the earth's surface is covered by water _____

Many people are surprised when they learn the answer _____ Water covers

more than two-thirds of the earth's surface _____ From the great oceans to the

smallest pond or stream, water is just about everywhere _____ However, do

we have enough water _____

Most of the earth's water is salt water, which is found in the oceans _____

Only a small part is fresh water, which is found in lakes, rivers, streams, and

ponds _____ This small supply of fresh water is very important _____ We use

fresh water for drinking and growing crops _____ Since the supply of fresh

water is small, humans must be careful to conserve water as well as keep the

fresh water free from pollution _____

10 Level 11/Unit 1

Extension: Have students write a paragraph on how they can conserve water at home.

1

Macmillan/McGraw-Hill

WHAT ARE THE FOUR TYPES OF SENTENCES?

A **sentence** is a group of words that expresses a complete thought. The four types of sentences are statement, question, command, and exclamation. A **statement** tells something. A **question** asks something. A **command** tells someone to do something. An **exclamation** expresses strong feeling.

Read each sentence. Write *S* in the blank if the sentence is a statement. Write *Q* if it is a question. Write *C* if it is a command. Write *E* if it is an exclamation.

1. _____ Sarah's great-grandfather was a fisherman in Norway.

2. _____ Do you know in what year he was born?

3. _____ Look on the back of the photograph on the mantel.

4. _____ It says "Ragnar Nilsson, born 1901."

5. _____ Did Sarah tell you the name of the town where her grandfather lived?

6. _____ Is the name of the city Stavanger?

7. _____ Yes, I think it is.

8. _____ What a beautiful town it is!

9. _____ Sarah told me she would like to visit Norway someday.

10. _____ She would like to see the country where her ancestors lived.

11. _____ Many Norwegians work on fishing boats.

12. _____ A popular kind of fish to eat is herring.

13. _____ Norwegians prepare this single fish in hundreds and hundreds of different ways!

14. _____ I tasted pickled herring at Sarah's Christmas party last year.

15. _____ The theme of Sarah's party was "A Taste of Norway."

Extension: Have students choose five of the sentences in the exercise and rewrite them as different types of sentences. Then have them identify what type of sentence each new sentence is.

2

Level 11/Unit 1

15

Macmillan/McGraw-Hill

Statements and Questions

A **statement** is a sentence that tells something. It ends with a period. (.) A **question** is a sentence that asks something. It ends with a question mark. (**?**)

Read each sentence. Add the correct end punctuation to each sentence. Then rewrite the sentence as a question if it is a statement. Rewrite the sentence as a statement if it is a question.

1. Has your sister been on a sailboat

_____

2. His sister sailed in a race across the lake

_____

3. Is the mast on that sailboat tall

_____

4. Did we go sailing on Lake Erie with your uncle last summer

_____

5. Devin's uncle learned to sail in the navy

_____

6. That sailboat has a small motor on it for emergencies

_____

7. Is the name of your uncle's sailboat *Roberta*

_____

8. Did it take longer than two hours to paint your uncle's boat

_____

9. You washed the boat before you painted it

_____

10. She is very excited about going sailing next weekend

_____

Macmillan/McGraw-Hill

Extension: Have students work in pairs, one writing questions about a particular hobby and the other answering the questions with written statements.

COMMANDS AND EXCLAMATIONS

A **command** is a sentence that gives an order. It ends with a period. (.) An **exclamation** is a sentence that shows strong feeling. It ends with an exclamation mark. (**!**)

Read each sentence. If the sentence is a command, write *C* in the blank. If it is an exclamation, write *E*. If the sentence is not a command or an exclamation, write *N.*

1. _____ My goodness, what a storm!

2. _____ The lightning is so brilliant!

3. _____ Shut the window.

4. _____ Make sure all the windows in the house are closed.

5. _____ Has anybody seen the cat since the storm began?

6. _____ That thunderclap was so loud it almost broke my eardrums!

7. _____ Max is afraid of thunder, you know.

8. _____ There he is!

9. _____ We saw him hiding behind the couch.

10. _____ The wind is very strong.

11. _____ Wow, the wind just broke off a branch from that tree!

12. _____ The cat ran toward the basement.

13. _____ I tried to comfort the poor cat.

14. _____ Hold the cat.

15. _____ If the lights do go out, Max will have an advantage over us.

16. _____ Explain what you mean.

17. _____ Are you talking about cats having nine lives?

18. _____ Cats can see in the dark because their eyes let in more light.

19. _____ Oh no, the lights just went out!

20. _____ Give the cat some water, please.

Extension: Have students write a short description of a storm they have experienced. Ask them to include and label at least two commands and two exclamations.

4

Level 11/Unit 1

20

Macmillan/McGraw-Hill

FOUR TYPES OF SENTENCES

There are four types of sentences. A **statement** tells something. It ends with a period. A **question** asks something. It ends with a question mark. A **command** tells someone to do something. It ends with a period. An **exclamation** shows strong feeling. It ends with an exclamation mark.

Imagine that you are on a cruise to a part of the world you have always wanted to visit. Write a letter to your best friend describing the ship, the places you have seen, and the people you have met. Use at least one of each type of sentence. Write *S* next to a statement, *Q* next to a question, *C* next to a command, and *E* next to an exclamation. Be sure to use correct end punctuation for each sentence.

_____

_____

_____

_____

_____

_____

_____

_____

_____

_____

_____

_____

_____

_____

_____

_____

Macmillan/McGraw-Hill

Extension: Have students exchange letters with a partner and rewrite four sentences in the letter as other types of sentences.

SUBJECTS AND PREDICATES

Rewrite the paragraph below. Complete each fragment in the paragraph by adding a subject or predicate to it.

Many different ways to cook eggs. Boil, fry, scramble, poach, make an omelet. Like most kinds of eggs. Grandmother's favorite way of cooking eggs. Scrambled eggs with mushrooms, cheese, tomatoes, and a dash of oregano. Use eggs to make cakes and cookies, too! A woman we called the "Egg Lady." Raised chickens. Delivered eggs to everyone in our neighborhood. Fresh eggs. Today our family. Gets eggs at the grocery store.

_____

_____

_____

_____

_____

_____

_____

_____

_____

_____

_____

_____

_____

_____

_____

_____

_____

_____

Macmillan/McGraw-Hill

6 | **Extension:** Have students, working in pairs, take turns writing fragments and completing them. |

COMPLETE/SIMPLE SUBJECTS

Every sentence has two main parts, a subject and a predicate. A **complete subject** is all the words in a sentence that tell what or whom the sentence is about. A **simple subject** is the main word in the complete subject.

Example: *All of the students in Ms. Brown's class* went to see the play.
The complete subject is in italic type. The simple subject is *students*.

Read each sentence. Draw a line under the complete subject. Then circle the simple subject.

1. Countless folktales began in America.

2. Different regions have different stories.

3. A favorite folktale character is Paul Bunyan.

4. This character was a giant lumberjack.

5. Babe, a gigantic blue ox, helped Paul move trees.

6. Paul Bunyan's breakfast would amaze you!

7. The mighty lumberjack ranged throughout the Great Lakes region.

8. Another character from America's folktales is Joe Majarac.

9. Pennsylvania steel workers told stories about Joe.

10. Many Pittsburgh steel workers were immigrants from eastern Europe.

11. Joe was finally melted down to make the finest batch of steel ever made!

12. Many people have heard the stories and tall tales of John Henry.

13. This steel-driving man was a real person.

14. The real John Henry worked on a railroad construction crew in West Virginia during the 1800s.

15. John Henry's story is told also in a famous African-American song.

16. This well-known song describes a competition between John Henry and a mechanical drill.

17. The inventor of the mechanical drill challenged John Henry.

18. John Henry's mighty efforts defeated the mechanical drill.

36 Level 11/Unit 1

Extension: Have students write a summary of a tall tale they enjoy. Have them underline the complete subjects and circle the simple subjects.

7

Macmillan/McGraw-Hill

COMPLETE/SIMPLE PREDICATES

As you have learned, every sentence has a subject and a predicate. A **complete predicate** is all the words in the sentence that tell what the subject does or is. A **simple predicate** is the main word in the complete predicate.

   The Marching Band *played two songs before the game.*

The complete predicate is in italic type. The simple predicate is *played*.

Read each fragment. Turn the fragment into a sentence by adding a complete predicate. Then circle the simple predicate in the words you have added.

1. Farm families that lived a hundred years ago

_____

2. The children in the farm family

_____

3. Milking the cows twice a day

_____

4. The youngest children

_____

5. The pigs

_____

6. By springtime, the sun

_____

7. The wool

_____

8. The cows in the pasture

_____

9. Planting the year's crops

_____

8

Extension: Have students write a short description of farm life from an animal's point of view. Then have them underline the complete predicates and circle the simple predicates.

Level 11/Unit 1

18

Macmillan/McGraw-Hill

FRAGMENTS

When a sentence does not have either a subject or a predicate, it is a **fragment**. A fragment does not express a complete thought. A fragment can be corrected by adding the missing subject or predicate.

Read each sentence. Write *S* beside it if it is a sentence. Write *F* beside it if it is a fragment. Then rewrite the fragments correctly by adding a subject or a predicate.

1. _____ Hiked in the woods last weekend.

_____

2. _____ Most people are helpful to others.

_____

3. _____ Found two nickels and a quarter on the sidewalk.

_____

4. _____ My grade on the spelling test.

_____

5. _____ Never expected to meet her grandfather at the zoo.

_____

6. _____ Don't make a sound.

_____

7. _____ Got a job at the music store.

_____

8. _____ She studied the photographs in the album.

_____

9. _____ The adventure movie that we saw.

_____

10. _____ Ran quickly back to the garage.

_____

Macmillan/McGraw-Hill

20 Level 11/Unit 1

Extension: Have students write fragments and give them to partners to correct.

9

SUBJECTS AND PREDICATES

Every sentence must have a **subject** and a **predicate**. A **complete subject** is the words in the sentence that tell what or whom the sentence is about. A **complete predicate** is all the words in the sentence that tell what the subject is or does. A **fragment** is a group of words that is missing either a subject or a predicate. It does not express a complete thought.

Living in the country is different from living in the city. Write a paragraph about some of the differences between city life and country life. Underline all the complete subjects and circle all the complete predicates. Write *S* above each simple subject. Write *P* above each simple predicate.

_____

_____

_____

_____

_____

_____

_____

_____

_____

_____

_____

_____

_____

_____

_____

_____

_____

_____

_____

10   **Extension:** Have students identify complete and simple subjects and predicates in a newspaper or magazine article.

Macmillan/McGraw-Hill

COMPOUND SUBJECTS AND PREDICATES

Read the paragraphs. Then rewrite by combining sentences to make the paragraphs read more smoothly.

Gerald has a good imagination. He also draws very well. He described an incredible space station. He drew a picture of it, too. The space station had four separate living areas. It ran on solar power.

Have you ever invented an imaginary place? Have you ever written about the place? Invent a place. Describe it on a tape recorder.

Books can take you away to imaginary places. Pictures can take you there, too. Some authors write their books. Some illustrate them as well. C.S. Lewis is a famous creator of an imaginary land. J.R.R. Tolkien is another. *The Hobbit* is one of Tolkien's popular books. *The Lord of the Rings* is another. So is *Farmer Giles of Ham*. Richard read *The Chronicles of Narnia* by C.S. Lewis and loved them. I did, too.

_____

_____

_____

_____

_____

_____

_____

_____

_____

_____

_____

_____

_____

_____

_____

_____

Macmillan/McGraw-Hill

Level 11/Unit 1

Extension: Have students underline the subjects and circle the verbs in the paragraphs they wrote.

11

COMPOUND SUBJECTS

> A **compound subject** is two or more simple subjects that have the same predicate.
> The simple subjects are joined by *and* or *or*.

C.S. Lewis says in "The Voyage of the *Dawn Treader*" that most people have an imaginary country. Describe your imaginary country. Use at least four compound subjects in your description. Underline these compound subjects.

_____

_____

_____

_____

_____

_____

_____

_____

_____

_____

_____

_____

_____

_____

_____

_____

_____

_____

_____

_____

_____

_____

12   **Extension:** Have students identify compound subjects on a page of one of their books.

Level 11/Unit 1

Macmillan/McGraw-Hill

COMPOUND PREDICATES

> A **compound predicate** is two or more simple predicates that have the
> same subject. The simple predicates are joined by *and* or *or*.

Read each sentence. Draw a line under each compound predicate. Some
sentences do not have a compound predicate.

1. Have you ever wished you could talk to animals?

2. Of course, animals don't talk or communicate the way humans do.

3. Researchers and scientists tell us that animals have their own way of
   communicating.

4. Bees communicate with other bees and lead them to sources of food.

5. Can you guess how they do this?

6. Bees wiggle their bodies and perform a special dance in the air.

7. In this way, they communicate and act out the directions to the food source.

8. Another animal, the cat, purrs and rubs against a person's leg.

9. Purring means the cat is feeling happy and contented.

10. A cat rubs against a person's leg to show that it belongs to that person.

Complete each sentence by writing a compound predicate.

11. Cats _____ all sorts of little animals.

12. My aunt's cat _____.

13. One time, her cat _____.

14. My aunt _____.

15. "Cats _____," said my aunt.

15   Level 11/Unit 1

Extension: Have students write a short dialog between a cat and a mouse, using
at least three compound predicates.

13

Macmillan/McGraw-Hill

COMPOUND SUBJECTS AND PREDICATES

> A **compound subject** is two or more simple subjects with the same predicate.
>
> A **compound predicate** is two or more simple predicates with the same subject.

Read each sentence. Then follow the instructions for each one.

1. Amber plays the flute in the school orchestra. (rewrite the sentence using a compound predicate)

   _____

2. She learned a difficult piece and played it as a solo in the fall program. (rewrite the sentence as two sentences)

   _____

3. Her parents were very proud of her. (rewrite the sentence using a compound subject)

   _____

4. The school's music groups rehearse three times a week. (rewrite the sentence using a compound subject and compound predicate)

   _____

5. Rock is one of Amber's favorite kinds of music. (rewrite the sentence using a compound subject)

   _____

6. Amber and her brothers formed a music group. (rewrite the sentence using a compound predicate)

   _____

7. The people at the senior citizens' center clapped after the performance. (rewrite the sentence using a compound subject and compound predicate)

   _____

8. Are a recording career and great fame in Amber's future? (rewrite the sentence as two sentences)

   _____

Extension: Ask students to write a paragraph about something they would like to do some day. Have them use a compound subject and compound predicate in at least one sentence.

14

Level 11/Unit 1

8

Macmillan/McGraw-Hill

SENTENCE COMBINING WITH COMPOUND SUBJECTS AND PREDICATES

Short sentences with the same subject or the same predicate can be combined using *and*.

Read each set of sentences. Rewrite them, combining them to make one new sentence. Then underline each compound subject and circle each compound predicate.

1. The *Dawn Treader* has a dragon head. It looks very much like a Viking ship.

___ _____

___ _____

2. The Vikings lived in northern Europe. They were fearless sailors.

___ _____

___ _____

3. The coast of Canada has ancient Viking settlements. So does southern Russia.

___ _____

___ _____

4. The brave Viking sailors set out on the open ocean in their small boats. They explored much of the world.

___ _____

___ _____

5. Today's Swedes are descended from the Vikings. So are the Danes. The Norwegians are also descendants of the Vikings.

___ _____

___ _____

Macmillan/McGraw-Hill

Extension: Have students exchange descriptions and underline the compound subjects and predicates. If there are none, have the students work together to rewrite several sentences with compound subjects and predicates.

COMPOUND SENTENCES

Read the paragraph. Underline each compound sentence that uses *and, or,* or *but* to connect complete thoughts.

> Australia, home of the Great Barrier Reef, is one of the most interesting countries in the world. Australia has fascinating cities, deserts, and rain forests, and many of its unusual animals exist nowhere else on earth. Everyone knows about the kangaroo, but did you know that the wallaby is the kangaroo's smaller cousin? Another unusual Australian mammal is the echidna, also known as the spiny anteater. This animal is covered with sharp quills like a porcupine, and it is active only at night. The duck-billed platypus is a mammal, but this small creature lays eggs like a bird! Hikers in the desert have to be careful, or they may step right on a Thorny Devil lizard. And what might you see sleeping high in a eucalyptus tree? It's a fat, lazy koala taking a nap!

Write a paragraph about an unusual animal you have seen in a zoo, aquarium, or nature film. Use five compound sentences.

_____

_____

_____

_____

_____

_____

_____

_____

_____

_____

_____

_____

_____

Extension: Have students rewrite each compound sentence in the paragraph as two shorter sentences.

Macmillan/McGraw-Hill

WHAT ARE COMPOUND SENTENCES?

A **compound sentence** contains two sentences joined by *and, or,* or *but.* These words are called conjunctions. Compound sentences express more than one complete thought.

Circle the number of each sentence that expresses more than one complete thought.

1. An aquarium is a kind of zoo just for fish and other sea animals.

2. Many cities in the U.S. have aquariums, and they are always popular attractions.

3. The New England Aquarium in Boston is one of the best known.

4. It has exhibits about different marine environments, and one of these is its new display about a coral reef.

5. Chicago is far away from the nearest ocean, but it also has a famous aquarium.

6. Shedd Aquarium, located on the shores of Lake Michigan, is one of the country's oldest.

7. Visitors to aquariums can observe many kinds of fish, or they can learn about sea mammals such as whales and dolphins.

8. Fish, mammals, and reptiles share the marine environment.

9. So far, people and marine animals have been able to live together, but the survival of many kinds of marine animals is threatened by pollution.

10. Perhaps your family can visit an aquarium someday.

Write two sentences on a topic of your choice. Use *and, or,* or *but* in each sentence.

1. _____

_____

2. _____

_____

Macmillan/McGraw-Hill

Extension: Have students exchange sentences with a partner and rewrite each compound sentence as two shorter ones.

COMPOUND SENTENCES WITH *AND/OR/BUT*

Use a comma before the words *and, or,* or *but* when you write a compound sentence.

Read each sentence. Follow the instructions for each one.

1. Camels were introduced into Australia from Afghanistan. They have adapted very well to the new environment. (combine the sentences using the word *and*)

   _____

   _____

2. Camels have adapted to life in the Australian desert. They are not native to this area. (combine the sentences using the word *but*)

   _____

   _____

3. Hold on tight when you ride on a camel. You might find yourself thrown off! (combine the sentences using the word *or*)

   _____

   _____

4. One of two types of camels, dromedaries come from Arabia. Bactrians are native to central Asia. (combine the sentences using the word *and*)

   _____

   _____

5. Dromedary camels have one hump. Bactrian camels have two humps. (combine the sentences using the word *and*)

   _____

   _____

6. Visitors to Australia can fly into the country. They can arrive by boat. (combine the sentences using the word *or*)

   _____

   _____

Macmillan/McGraw-Hill

SENTENCE COMBINING

Short sentences can be combined with a **conjunction** to form compound sentences.

Imagine that you are on a dive in the Great Barrier Reef. All around are colorful fish, strange creatures, and the huge coral reef. Write a description of what you can see and feel under the sea. Include five compound sentences, joined by the words *and, or,* and *but,* in your description.

_____

_____

_____

_____

_____

_____

_____

_____

_____

_____

_____

_____

_____

_____

_____

_____

_____

_____

_____

Macmillan/McGraw-Hill

RUN-ON SENTENCES

> A **run-on sentence** joins together two or more sentences that should be written as separate sentences.

Fix each run-on sentence by breaking it into shorter sentences. Add capital letters and punctuation marks where needed.

1. The library is presenting a program next week and it's about coral reefs and I'm definitely going to the program.

   _____

   _____

2. The speaker at the program will be a professor from the university and she has studied the reef and even written a book about it.

   _____

   _____

3. The program starts at 7:30 and I'm going to have to hurry to make it but I think my dad can give me a ride to the library after dinner.

   _____

   _____

4. Last month I went to a program about bats at the library and it was great and I learned how helpful bats are to people.

   _____

   _____

5. A lot of people think bats are horrible but they don't understand that bats eat harmful insects and if they didn't, there would be a lot more mosquitoes.

   _____

   _____

6. I found several books about bats and I checked them out and I decided to build a bat house for our backyard.

   _____

20 **Extension:** Have students write a paragraph about a nature program they have seen on television. Ask them to use several compound sentences.

Level 11/Unit 1

6

Macmillan/McGraw-Hill

NOUNS

Read the paragraph. Underline each word that names a person, place, thing, or idea. Above each underlined word, write *Pe* if it names a person. Write *Pl* if it names a place. Write *Th* if it names a thing. Write *Id* if it names an idea.

Some people who help others are famous. Some examples are

Mother Teresa and Nelson Mandela, who both won the Nobel Peace

Prize. But most people who are a help to others are not famous. The girl

who delivers your newspaper might be very helpful to her neighbors.

The man you meet at the grocery store might do volunteer work at the

local hospital. Volunteers and other helpful people get satisfaction from

assisting others. It makes them feel good if they are making a

contribution to the happiness of others. Look around. Helpful citizens

are everywhere!

Now look at the chart. Cross out each word that does not belong in the category where it is placed.

Persons	farmer baby	Aunt Lucy elephant	general Mariah Carey
Places	room pencil	school Australia	Cleveland gymnasium
Things	hammer tiger	Eiffel Tower weather	glove sister
Ideas	patriotism joy	democracy Judaism	vice president football

Macmillan/McGraw-Hill

Extension: Have students quiz each other by making a list of ten words and having a partner circle the nouns in the list.

WHAT IS A NOUN?

A **noun** names a person, place, thing, or idea.

Read each sentence. Fill in the blank with a noun.

1. There are many ways kids can help other _____ _____.

2. My friends and I wanted to donate some _____ to

   _____.

3. We had read about all the damage caused by a hurricane in the state of

   _____.

4. _____ said we should do something to help.

5. We tried to think of a _____ to earn some money.

6. The best _____ was to have a pet wash.

7. I asked Ms. Thomas if we could have it at the _____ _____.

8. _____ gave us permission to have it there.

9. The day we chose was _____ _____.

10. The _____ before, we gathered all the

    _____ we would need.

11. Sheila volunteered to bring _____ and soap.

12. Donyell's _____ helped us set up the signs.

13. Luckily for us, the weather report called for a warm, sunny _____ __.

14. At nine o'clock, the first _____ arrived.

15. It wasn't easy washing all those _____ __.

16. According to Jason, we washed 32 _____ in eight hours.

17. We all had a feeling of satisfaction when we counted the _____ __.

18. We were able to send more than $120 to _____ _.

19. We even saved money for a special _____ _.

20. We went to _____ for dinner afterward!

Extension: Have students write above each word they have added whether it
names a person, place, thing, or idea.

Macmillan/McGraw-Hill

COMMON NOUNS

A **common noun** names any person, place, thing, or idea.

Circle each common noun in the list. Then use some of the words you have circled to write a paragraph about ways young people can help their communities.

adult	ill	ignore	book	happiness
often	girl	day care center	survive	entertainment
assist	Martin Luther King, Jr.	school	music	clever
volunteer	satisfaction	parent	home	birthday
Americans	card	loneliness	eat	Riverside Hospital

_____

_____

_____

_____

_____

_____

_____

_____

_____

_____

_____

_____

_____

_____

_____

_____

_____

_____

_____

_____

Macmillan/McGraw-Hill

15   Level 11/Unit 2

Extension: Have students work in pairs to read a newspaper or magazine article and circle all the common nouns.

23

PROPER NOUNS

| A **proper noun** names a **particular** person, place, thing, or idea. A proper noun begins with a capital letter. |

Write a proper noun that names an example of each common noun.

1. building _____

2. professional athlete or entertainer _____

3. car_____

4. university_____

5. relative_____

6. quality_____

7. store_____

8. religion_____

9. month_____

10. company_____

Read the paragraph. Capitalize each proper noun by drawing three lines under the first letter. The first one is capitalized for you.

   If you asked someone to name the world's most helpful person, many names would come to mind. One of them would certainly be Mother Teresa. This elderly nun has helped the poor of calcutta,india, for more than fifty years. She was born in the small country of albania in europe and went to india as a young woman. There she decided to help the street people of the city. Her work became known around the world, and mother teresa gained the respect of millions. Her admirers include john paul II, the leader of the catholic church. She won the nobel prize in 1979. She wore her blue-and-white nun's habit when she accepted the famous award in stockholm, sweden.

Extension: Have students work in pairs, one student naming a proper noun, such as George Washington, and the other a common noun that names what the proper noun is—for example, president.

Macmillan/McGraw-Hill

TITLES AND ABBREVIATIONS

An **abbreviation** is a shortened form of a word.

Read the sentences. Fill in each blank with an abbreviation from the list.

Ms.   Ph. D.   Rev.   Dr.   Gov.   Mr.   U.S.   Mrs.   M.D.   P.M.

1. The sign on the surgeon's door said Marta Ramirez, _____.

2. The woman in charge of the art show is _____ Morrison.

3. Shawna's dream is to meet _____ Clinton, the

   President's wife.

4. The three biggest _____ auto companies are Ford,

   Chrysler, and General Motors.

5. The new minister at our church is _____ Laura Tan.

6. Tamara is taking a gymnastics class at 3:00 _____.

7. _____ Branstad of Iowa is a Republican.

8. That man with the softball is the coach, _____ Fortunato.

9. The nurse said that _____ Singh would see me now.

10. Christopher Palmer, _____, is the director of the

    counseling center.

Spell out each abbreviation.

11. On her trip to New York City, Monica got to visit the UN _____.

12. All my friends call my mom Dr. Anderson _____.

13. Gen. Dwight Eisenhower was later elected president of the United States

    _____.

14. Send the letter to your senator in Washington, D.C. _____

15. The Roman Empire collapsed in the year A.D. 476. _____

Macmillan/McGraw-Hill

Extension: Have students write a short newspaper article on a recent school
event. Have them use at least three abbreviations in their articles.

PLURAL NOUNS

Read each sentence. Underline each word that names more than one person, place, thing, or idea.

1. One thing I really like about my town is looking in the store windows.

2. It seems like there are always interesting items to look at.

3. On Sunday mornings, I sometimes take a walk with my dad.

4. My younger brothers come, too.

5. The streets are always very quiet on Sunday morning.

6. During the week, big trucks make a lot of noise.

7. We live about three blocks from the center of town.

8. It only takes a few minutes to walk there.

9. I like to walk past the big houses on Park Street.

10. One of them, a red brick house, is four stories high.

11. It has three porches, many windows, and several huge bushes.

12. One of the many trees in the yard is a buckeye tree.

13. In the fall, I like to collect the shiny brown nuts.

14. My parents know the woman who lives there, but I've never met her.

15. After a short walk, we come to a small store that sells office supplies.

16. In the window are pens, paper, and little notebooks.

17. Around the corner is one of my favorite spots in town.

18. Our town has two bookstores, and this one is my favorite.

19. The one I like always has displays of the latest books.

20. It's fun to daydream about all the different places described in the books.

Macmillan/McGraw-Hill

26 **Extension:** Have students make lists of some of the interesting things they might see in their downtown. Have them circle each plural noun they list.

Level 11/Unit 2   25

WHAT IS A PLURAL NOUN?

A **plural noun** names more than one person, place, thing, or idea.

Rewrite each sentence, changing each underlined word to its plural form. Make any other changes necessary to make your new sentence correct.

1. The hillside above the town is dotted with trees and hedges.

_____

_____

2. A songbird is singing high up in the oak tree.

_____

_____

3. An automobile speeds around the corner and disappears up a side street.

_____

_____

4. The small house by the stream is awfully cute.

_____

5. A park in the neighborhood is a gathering spot for everyone.

_____

_____

6. A holiday is always very busy at our house.

_____

7. I don't understand how we missed the sign for the railroad station.

_____

_____

8. Do you have any idea where this road leads?

_____

Macmillan/McGraw-Hill

Extension: Have students work in pairs. One student lists five nouns; the other writes their plural forms. Then they reverse tasks.

PLURAL NOUNS WITH -S AND -ES

To form plural nouns: Add -s to most nouns.

  student—students   bike—bikes

Add -es to nouns ending in s, ch, sh, or x.

  dress—dresses   watch—watches

Write the plural of each noun. Then write a paragraph on a topic that interests you. Use at least five of the words you have written.

1. box _____
2. fruit _____
3. splash _____
4. gas _____
5. church _____
6. mix _____
7. tree _____
8. ditch _____
9. bicycle _____
10. acorn _____

11. brush _____
12. patch _____
13. cloud _____
14. fox _____
15. color _____
16. player _____
17. bush _____
18. guess _____
19. jacket _____
20. batch _____

_____

_____

_____

_____

_____

_____

_____

_____

Extension: Have students scan a newspaper article and circle each singular noun.
Then have them write the plural of each noun they have circled.

Macmillan/McGraw-Hill

PLURAL NOUNS WITH *-IES* AND *-EYS*

To form the plural of nouns ending in a consonant and *y*, change *y* to *i* and add *-es*. To form the plural of nouns ending in a vowel and *y*, add *-s*.

Write the plural of each word. Then write a letter to a friend about the town or city where you live. Describe how it looks, what you like or dislike about it, and some interesting things you might see on a walk. Use at least five of the plural nouns you wrote.

1. party _____
2. donkey _____
3. worry _____
4. penny _____
5. day _____
6. valley _____
7. city _____
8. puppy _____
9. baby _____
10. toy _____

11. strawberry _____
12. pony _____
13. lady _____
14. fly _____
15. jelly _____
16. factory _____
17. story _____
18. journey _____
19. play _____
20. spy _____

_____
_____
_____
_____
_____
_____
_____
_____

Macmillan/McGraw-Hill

Extension: Have students quiz each other by writing sentences that incorrectly use singular nouns instead of plural nouns. The partner must supply the correct plural form.

SPECIAL PLURAL NOUNS

Some nouns have special plural forms.

Solve the crossword puzzle using the clues. Then choose any six words in the puzzle and use each one in a different sentence.

Across

3. You use these to walk

6. They say "Honk, honk"

7. They pulled covered wagons across the prairie

8. Little boys and girls

Down

1. What boys grow up to be

2. Cheese lovers

4. We use them for chewing

5. What girls grow up to be

1. _____

2. _____

3. _____

4. _____

5. _____

6. _____

30 Extension: Have students create another crossword puzzle using any plurals in this unit.

Level 11/Unit 2 **14**

Macmillan/McGraw-Hill

Name: _____   Date: _____

MORE PLURAL NOUNS

A **plural noun** names more than one person, place, thing, or idea.

What kinds of things might you see if you visited the Mexican countryside?
Circle the plural nouns in the following paragraph.

I loved my visit to Mexico. When we drove through the
countryside, we saw farmers digging potatoes and
harvesting corn. We wore our new ponchos, but the
workers were already sweaty from working hard in the sun.
Soon they would drop their hoes on the ground and rest.
Along all the roadsides were stands where children were
selling many kinds of fruit. We bought some fruit and had
enough for three lunches that week. I want to visit Mexico
again soon. It's such a beautiful country. One week there
just wasn't long enough.

Macmillan/McGraw-Hill

Extension: Have students write a paragraph about a trip they took. Have them
use at least five plural nouns.

NOUNS THAT FORM PLURALS BY CHANGING
-*F* OR -*FE* TO -*VES*

To form the plural of some nouns ending in -*f* or -*fe*, change the -*f* to -*v* and add -*es* or -*s*. Add -*s* to other nouns ending in -*f* or -*fe*.
    loaf   *loaves*   half   *halves*

Write the plural form of each noun. Then write a sentence below using each plural form.

1. life _____

2. roof _____

3. shelf _____

4. chief _____

5. elf _____

6. gulf _____

7. safe _____

8. cliff _____

9. wolf _____

10. knife _____

11. _____

12. _____

13. _____

14. _____

15. _____

16. _____

17. _____

18. _____

19. _____

20. _____

Extension: Have students circle each word that changes *f* to *v* when forming a plural and underline each one that retains the *f*.

Macmillan/McGraw-Hill

NOUNS THAT FORM PLURALS BY CHANGING
-O TO -OS OR -OES

To form the plural of nouns that end with a **vowel** and -*o*, add -*s*. To form the plural of nouns that end with a **consonant** and -*o*, add -*s* or -*es*.

rodeo	*rodeos*	solo	*solos*	tornado	*tornadoes*

Read each sentence. Cross out each incorrect plural. Write the correct plural on the line. If the sentence is correct, write *C* on the line.

1. The men were working in groups of twoes and threes. _____

2. The were digging with shovels and hos. _____

3. Ted helped the men dig their potatos. _____

4. The sun warmed Ted from his head to his toes. _____

5. The tomatoes were red and juicy. _____

6. The boys wore ponchoes to keep warm. _____

7. Potatoes grow under the ground. _____

8. Carmen played her guitar and sang several soloes. _____

9. Please put the shovels and hoes in the shed. _____

10. I think that drawings in a book are nicer than photoes. _____

11. Rodeos are popular in Mexico. _____

12. The family enjoyed a meal of tacoes and corn. _____

13. She arranged the yo-yos in rows by color. _____

14. Which cities in Mexico have zoos? _____

15. Name the heros of your favorite books. _____

Macmillan/McGraw-Hill

SPECIAL PLURAL NOUNS

> Some nouns have singular and plural forms that are the same.
>   moose   *moose*   deer   *deer*
>
> Some plural nouns have special forms.
>   child   *children*   woman   *women*

Write *C* after each sentence that uses the correct plural form. Rewrite each sentence that uses an incorrect form.

1. A walk in the country is a good way to see lots of animals.

   _____

2. If you're quiet as you walk, you can surprise quail in the forest.

   _____

3. Sheeps aren't wild animals, but you can often see them in the country.

   _____

4. In most midwestern states, you are likely to see gooses migrating in the fall of the year.

   _____

5. Salmons struggle against the river's current in spawning season.

   _____

6. There's a herd of deer in the park near my house.

   _____

7. Wolves sometimes hunt large animals like mooses.

   _____

8. Several children crossed the street at the same time.

   _____

9. We had problems with mouses getting into the birdseed.

   _____

10. Bears have large tooths.

   _____

Extension: Have students work in pairs. One student will say a singular noun; the other will say the plural. After they have named ten nouns, they can reverse tasks. Encourage them to think of special plural forms.

Macmillan/McGraw-Hill

MORE PLURAL NOUNS

To form the plural of some nouns ending in *-f* or *-fe,* change the *-f* to *-v* and add *-es* or *-s.* Add *-s* to other nouns ending in *-f* or *-fe.* To form the plural of nouns that end with a vowel and *-o,* add **-s.** To form the plural of nouns that end with a consonant and *-o,* add **-s** or **-es.** A few nouns have the same form in the singular and in the plural.

Having friends is more important than having money. Write a story about someone who learns an important lesson. Use plural nouns correctly in your story.

_____

_____

_____

_____

_____

_____

_____

_____

_____

_____

_____

_____

_____

_____

_____

_____

_____

_____

_____

_____

_____

Macmillan/McGraw-Hill

Extension: Have students make a set of 20 flash cards with ten singular nouns from this section and ten of their own choosing. They should write the correct plural on the back of each card.

POSSESSIVE NOUNS

A **possessive noun** is a noun that shows who or what owns or has something.

Storms can be pretty scary. Read the following paragraph. Circle the possessive nouns.

Mom had gone to the children's daycare center to pick

up Ned. I was sitting on the porch swing reading with one eye

and watching our puppies' antics with the other. As I glanced

up, I saw the funnel cloud. "Twister!" I yelled. But my brother's

radio was blaring so loud that he couldn't hear me. When I

looked again, I was horrified to see that our house was

directly in the tornado's path. The sky's increasing darkness

was frightening. I raced up the stairs to the landing and

screamed again, "Josh, for heaven's sake, look out the

window!" This time he heard me. Safe in the basement, we

listened to the storm's roar. I was glad Josh had grabbed our

parents' flashlight as he dashed past their room. It was pitch

dark down there!

36
Extension: Write a paragraph about Mom and Ned. Exchange paragraphs with a partner and circle each possessive noun.

Level 11/Unit 2

8

Macmillan/McGraw-Hill

WHAT IS A POSSESSIVE NOUN?

A **possessive noun** is a noun that shows who or what owns or has something.
puppy   *puppy's*   Josh   *Josh's*

Read each sentence. Circle each possessive noun. Then use each noun in a sentence of your own.

1. Shannon heard her mother's voice.

_____

2. "Please shut the windows in your brother's room!" she called.

_____

3. Shannon was practicing chess and daydreaming about making her school's chess team.

_____

4. She remembered the chess coach's words to her.

_____

5. "I think you can be one of the team's strongest players," he said with a smile.

_____

6. Some of the game's rules were difficult to learn at first.

_____

7. But after several months' practice, Shannon had learned them by heart.

_____

8. Then Shannon heard her dad's voice.

_____

9. "It's starting to rain, Shannon," he said. "Didn't you hear Mom's request?"

_____

10. Jumping up from the chessboard, Shannon ran to her brother Robin's room and closed the window.

_____

Macmillan/McGraw-Hill

FORMING SINGULAR POSSESSIVE NOUNS

Add an apostrophe and an -s to a singular noun to make it possessive.
Shannon   *Shannon's*   storm   *storm's*

Write the possessive form of each noun. Then use the noun in a sentence.

1. student _____

_____

2. leaf _____

_____

3. summer _____

_____

4. Mr. Grover _____

_____

5. lion _____

_____

6. computer _____

_____

7. Sesame Street _____

_____

8. shoe _____

_____

9. book _____

_____

10. car _____

_____

Macmillan/McGraw-Hill

FORMING PLURAL POSSESSIVE NOUNS

Add an apostrophe to a plural noun that ends in -s to make it possessive.
  parents   *parents'*

Add an apostrophe and an -s to form the possessive of plural nouns that do not end in -s.
  children   *children's*

Read each sentence. Circle each plural noun. Then write the possessive form of each noun.

1. Laura and I watched the children play in the sandbox. _____

2. I'll never forget seeing the dolphins in Florida! _____

3. The shearer came to shear our flock of sheep yesterday. _____

4. Those are two of my favorite songs. _____

5. The owner of those buildings lives in California. _____

6. How many radios does your friend own? _____

7. We watched the men get off the train. _____

8. We counted 39 deer in the park last weekend. _____

9. Grandmother visited nine states on her trip. _____

10. Mom was the second-fastest of all the women. _____

Now write five sentences. In each sentence, use one of the plural possessive nouns you wrote above.

11. _____

12. _____

13. _____

14. _____

15. _____

Macmillan/McGraw-Hill

Extension: Have students draw a picture to illustrate one of the sentences they have written.

POSSESSIVE NOUNS

> A possessive noun shows who or what owns or has something.
> Add an apostrophe and an *-s* to a singular noun to make it possessive.
> Add an apostrophe to a plural noun that ends in *-s* to make it possessive.
> Add an apostrophe and an *-s* to form the possessive of plural nouns that do not end in *-s*.

Proofread the paragraph. Correct each incorrect possessive noun.

Our familys vacation was exciting this year. My two sisters and I went to the beach in August and stayed at Grandmothers house. We went swimming, snoozed in the sun, and looked for seashells. On the last night, my sisters radio was tuned to the weather station. The announcers voice said, "Hurricane warnings have been posted for the coastal area." Jennifer and Jane came running into the kitchen. Dad and I were washing the dishes. Jennifers voice was shaking. "What should we do?" she asked. "First, we'll ask Grandmas' advice," Dad answered. "Then we'll turn on the TV and try to find out more about this hurricane!" The hurricanes fury was spent before it reached us. It sure was the vacations' most exciting event, but Grandma remained pretty calm. I guess she is used to hurricanes.

Write the possessive form of each noun. Then use the possessive noun in a sentence of your own.

9. raccoon _____

_____

10. children _____

_____

11. fire truck _____

_____

12. jacket _____

_____

Extension: Have students change each of the singular possessives above to a plural and each plural possessive to a singular one. Then have them write five more sentences using the new words.

40

Level 11/Unit 2   16

Macmillan/McGraw-Hill

ACTION VERBS

Read the following paragraph. Notice the colorful words that express action and tell what happened. Underline these action verbs.

Fishing captures all of my attention and most of my time every summer. Every time I snap my rod back and release the line with my finger, I envision a bluegill. He flashes through the water in hot pursuit of my favorite spinner. The line plays out. I reel it in slowly and jerk it ever so slightly. Can I entice that small-mouthed panfish? Or maybe a bass will fly into the air and dive back into the water to shake off my hook. My mouth waters when I picture that fish in my pan. I'm hooked on fishing, for sure!

Macmillan/McGraw-Hill

Extension: Have students write a paragraph that describes a favorite game or sport. Remind them to use vivid action verbs.

WHAT IS AN ACTION VERB?

An **action verb** is a word that expresses action. It tells what the subject does or did.

Read each sentence. Underline each action verb.

1. Jessica won the spelling bee at school.

2. José captured a blue ribbon at the science fair.

3. Another boy played the piano very well.

4. Bakari defeated everyone in the class chess championship.

5. In her schoolwork, Mitsuyo earned straight A's.

6. Lawrence never missed one day of middle school.

7. For this perfect record, he received a certificate.

8. The principal congratulated him!

9. Jamal read more books than anybody in the reading contest.

10. My father mastered the sport of fishing at age ten.

On the line, write an action verb that makes sense in the sentence.

11. My mom _____ golf better than any of her friends.

12. Dad _____ the dog every morning.

13. David, my brother, _____ snow in the winter.

14. Even my grandmother _____ a trophy in a weightlifting contest.

15. I _____ experiments with my chemistry set.

Extension: Have students choose a paragraph from a book and write out each
action verb in it.

Macmillan/McGraw-Hill

ACTION VERBS WITH DIRECT OBJECTS

> A **direct object** is a noun or pronoun that receives the action of the verb. It answers the question *what?* or *whom?* after the verb.
>
> Jack loves *pizza*. Bill raced *Mark* to the corner.

Fill in each blank with an action verb that makes sense in the sentence.

1. It _____ lots of training to be good at sports.

2. Bakari _____ his wrists before casting his fishing line.

3. He also _____ the best bait on his hooks.

4. He finally _____ the biggest fish of the summer.

5. Hard work never _____ anybody!

Write a sentence using each word as the direct object of an action verb.

6. games _____

7. her_____

8. doctor _____

9. farms _____

10. you _____

11. octopus _____

12. me _____

13. police officer _____

14. them_____

15. Aunt Susan _____

Macmillan/McGraw-Hill

15 Level 11/Unit 3

Extension: Have students find the action verbs in a magazine or newspaper article. Discuss ways that colorful verbs make writing a paragraph more interesting.

43

MORE ACTION VERBS WITH DIRECT OBJECTS

> A **direct object** is a noun or pronoun that receives the action of the verb. It answers the question *what?* or *whom?* after the verb.

Read the paragraph. Fill in each blank with a word that makes sense in the sentence.

Our class wrote _____ to our favorite book authors. We had to

pick _____ we liked. The teacher gave us a

_____ to follow, but we also had to include our own

_____ . I've read many _____ , and I

admire several different _____ . I finally chose

_____ . This author wrote _____ . His

books really tell interesting _____ and contain fascinating

_____ . I used our class _____ . In the

letter I described _____ and my _____ .

My mom mailed my _____ yesterday on her way to work. I really

hope I receive an _____ !

Macmillan/McGraw-Hill

ACTION VERBS

Draw one line under each action verb and circle each direct object.

1. Bakari Lang's family supported him.

2. His brother offered tips on bass fishing.

3. Mr. Lang rented a boat on Lake Laurel.

4. One day after school, Bakari caught five fish.

5. After a while, Bakari rowed the boat to the dock.

6. On the day of the fishing contest, gray clouds covered the sun.

7. Bakari and his family ate breakfast.

8. Bakari caught his first fish.

9. He defeated five adults.

10. In the afternoon, a fish broke his line.

11. Bakari snared many fish.

12. Finally, Bakari hooked the championship fish.

Macmillan/McGraw-Hill

Extension: Have students write a paragraph about the food in the school cafeteria. Have them underline each action verb and circle each direct object they use.

PRESENT TENSE

> A verb in the **present** time or tense tells what happens now.
> I *tell* a story.

Think of an especially fun, exciting, or even scary time in your life. Write a
description of that time *as if it were happening again right now.* Try to make your
readers feel as if they are right there. Don't say "The soccer ball *headed* right
toward me!" Instead, say "The soccer ball *heads* right toward me!" Hear the
difference? Using present tense lets your readers feel like the story is
happening to them right now!

_____

_____

_____

_____

_____

_____

_____

_____

_____

_____

_____

_____

_____

_____

_____

_____

_____

_____

_____

Extension: Have students exchange paragraphs and underline the verbs that give
the reader a sense of being in the story.

Macmillan/McGraw-Hill

SINGULAR SUBJECTS: ADD -S OR -ES

When you use present-tense verbs with a singular subject, add -s to most verbs.

    happen   happens

Add -es to verbs that end in -s, -ch, -sh, -x, or -z.

    miss   misses;   pitch   pitches;   swish   swishes;   fizz   fizzes

Change y to i and add -es to verbs that end in a consonant and -y.

    hurry   hurries

Fill in the blank with the correct present-tense form of the verb in parentheses.

1. (snake) The old road _____ through the national park.

2. (push) A gray boulder _____ up like a humpback whale.

3. (grow) A large tree _____ near the river.

4. (arrive) My brother Sean _____ first at the place where we must set up camp.

5. (gaze) He _____ over the edge of the cliff.

6. (rush) Far below, the river _____ through a narrow channel.

7. (splash) A sheet of spray _____ up.

8. (worry) My friend Jenny _____ that she will lose her head.

9. (think) "I guess I will have to do my best," she _____ to herself.

10. (try) Jenny _____ to think how she will be able to get over her fear.

In the blank, write the present tense of a verb that makes sense in the sentence.

11. Shane _____ in the country on a farm.

12. His mother _____ as a nurse in a nearby town.

13. Shane's dad _____ corn, wheat, and soybeans.

14. Shane _____ his dad as much as he can.

15. He really _____ living in the country.

Extension: Have students find five examples of singular present-tense in one of their textbooks.

Macmillan/McGraw-Hill

PLURAL SUBJECTS: DO NOT ADD -S OR -ES

> Do not add -s or -es to a present-tense verb when the subject is plural or *I* or *you*.

Read each sentence. Complete the sentence with a present-tense verb that makes sense with the subject. Make sure you use the present tense.

1. Several hundred birds _____

2. I _____

3. The last houses on the street _____

4. Folklore and science fiction _____

5. The countries of Asia _____

6. The workers _____

7. My cousin and I _____

8. You _____

9. Wind and rain _____

10. Clouds _____

Write *C* next to each sentence that uses the correct form of the present tense. If the sentence is incorrect, write the correct verb form on the line.

11. Andrew and I shine our shoes every Sunday night. _____

12. You reads the newspaper often, don't you? _____

13. This is when the pirates digs up the treasure chest. _____

14. My grandparents give me a savings bond each year. _____

15. I needs a haircut soon. _____

Macmillan/McGraw-Hill

SINGULAR AND PLURAL SUBJECTS

> When you use present-tense verbs with a singular subject, add -s to most verbs.
>
> Add -es to verbs that end in -s, -ch, -sh, -x, or -z.
>
> Change y to i and add -es to verbs that end in a consonant and -y.
>
> Do not add -s or -es to a present-tense verb when the subject is plural or I or you.

Read each sentence. Write S in the blank if the subject is singular. Write P if it is plural.

_____ **1.** There are many books of fantasy and folktales.

_____ **2.** My favorite stories are about faraway lands.

_____ **3.** Toby loves adventure stories, especially books about animals.

_____ **4.** Wolves are the most interesting animals to Jan.

_____ **5.** The librarian is my best friend.

_____ **6.** Writers must have a lot of fun thinking up stories.

_____ **7.** Eve Bunting has written about her native country, Ireland.

_____ **8.** *Cricket* is a magazine that has great fiction.

_____ **9.** Some kids would rather read magazines than books.

_____ **10.** Writers are always readers, too.

Write a sentence using the correct present-tense form of the verb in parentheses.

11. (wonder, singular) _____

12. (put, plural) _____

13. (freeze, singular)_____

14. (forget, plural) _____

15. (hurt, singular) _____

Macmillan/McGraw-Hill

Extension: Have students select headlines from newspapers and write S or P (for Singular or Plural) over each present-tense verb.

PRESENT TENSE

Remember: when you use present-tense verbs with a singular subject, add -s to most verbs.

Add -es to verbs that end in -s, -ch, -sh, -x, or -z.
Change y to i and add -es to verbs that end in a consonant and -y.

Do not add -s or -es to a present-tense verb when the subject is plural or I or you.

Read the verbs in the list. Then write a paragraph using ten of the verbs in the present tense. Underline the verbs when you use them in your story.

swim	catch	rest	take	splash	eat	throw	dive
hold	watch	scream	go	want	join	talk	worry

_____

_____

_____

_____

_____

_____

_____

_____

_____

_____

_____

_____

_____

_____

_____

_____

_____

_____

Extension: Have students write sentences with the verbs they did not use in their paragraphs.

10

Macmillan/McGraw-Hill

PAST TENSE

A verb in the **past tense** tells what happened earlier.

Heard any good stories lately? Write a paragraph that describes a story you've read or movie you've seen recently. Tell about some of the characters and what happened to them, using at least ten past-tense verbs.

_____

_____

_____

_____

_____

_____

_____

_____

_____

_____

_____

_____

_____

_____

_____

_____

_____

_____

Macmillan/McGraw-Hill

10

Level 11/Unit 3

Extension: Have student pairs tell each other short narratives. When the storyteller uses a verb in the past tense, the listener should say "Stop." After ten "stops," the students switch roles.

VERBS IN THE PAST TENSE: ADD -ED

> Add -ed to most verbs to show past tense. If a verb ends with -e, drop the e and add -ed.
> work worked   shove shoved

Use the past tense of each verb in a sentence.

1. (wait) _____

2. (collect) _____

3. (divide) _____

4. (remember) _____

5. (call) _____

6. (twist) _____

7. (whisper) _____

8. (order) _____

9. (smile) _____

10. (shout) _____

Rewrite these sentences in the past tense.

11. My grandfather works on a fishing boat. _____

12. He steers the boat from the cabin. _____

13. He enjoys the long days out on the ocean. _____

14. He and his crew fish all along the east coast. _____

15. Grandma wants to move to Florida. _____

Extension: Have students write a short narrative describing in the past tense a
visit with their grandparents or other older relatives.

15

Macmillan/McGraw-Hill

VERBS IN THE PAST TENSE: CHANGE *Y* TO *I* AND ADD *-ED*

> To form the past tense of a verb ending with a consonant and *-y*, change the y to *i* and add *-ed*.
>
> dr*y*   dr*ied*   repl*y*   repl*ied*

Read each sentence. Circle the verb in parentheses that correctly completes the sentence.

1. Samantha (worried, worryed) that the flight would be late.

2. The rescue team (carried, carryed) the injured people to safety.

3. I (studyed, studied) harder for that test than I ever had before!

4. The mouse (scurried, scurryed) under the porch.

5. The pirates (pryed, pried) the lid off the old chest.

Read each sentence. Fill in the blank with the correct past-tense form of the verb in parentheses.

6. (bury) Crackers _____ the bone under the picnic table.

7. (marry) Rose's sister _____ the principal's son.

8. (rely) I felt proud when Mom said she _____ on me for support.

9. (cry) Chris _____ out for help.

10. (spy) Juan was angry when he found out his little sister and her friend

    _____ on him.

11. (try) The President _____ to come to some agreement.

12. (muddy) Philip's dad said his explanation _____ the water.

13. (apply) Jenny's sister _____ to college.

14. (hurry) Grandmother and I _____ to the bus stop.

15. (fry) Yoki and Toni _____ potatoes for the campers'

    breakfast.

Extension: Have students make a list of all the verbs they know that end in *-y* and change to *i* before adding *-ed*.

Macmillan/McGraw-Hill

VERBS IN THE PAST: DOUBLE THE FINAL CONSONANT AND ADD -ED

If a verb ends with one vowel and one consonant, double the consonant and add -ed to form the past tense.

mop   mop*ped*   bat   bat*ted*

Imagine that you are a doctor in a hospital emergency room. You have just spent a very busy night. Write your report about what happened during the night. Use five of the verbs on the following list in the past tense.

drop	jot	snag
grab	step	slip
stop	flop	hop
wrap	slam	jam

_____

_____

_____

_____

_____

_____

_____

_____

_____

_____

_____

_____

_____

_____

_____

_____

_____

54

Extension: Have students write sentences using five more verbs from the list in the past tense.

Level 11/Unit 3

5

Macmillan/McGraw-Hill

PAST TENSE

Add *-ed* to most verbs to show past tense.

If a verb ends with *-e*, drop the *e* and add *-ed.*

If a verb ends with a consonant and *-y*, change the *y* to *i* and add *-ed.*

If a verb ends with one vowel and one consonant, double the consonant and add *-ed.*

Read the paragraph. Cross out each incorrect verb tense form and write the correct one above it.

Brian needded to see the doctor last month. He sufferred from sore throats and coughs. His parents hopped he would get better, but he didn't. Finally, they caled the doctor and askked for an appointment. They arrivied at the hospital, and Brian waitted with his parents in the waiting room. The woman at the desk requiried Brian's parents to fill out some forms before he could see the doctor, and then he went into the office. The doctor ussed several different instruments to examine him. She lookked down his throat and presed down his tongue. She joted down a few notes on a form. Then she invitted Brian's parents into the examination room.

"Brian's problem is clear," she announcced.

"What is it?" Brian wonderred.

"Brian's tonsils will have to come out," the doctor told them.

Macmillan/McGraw-Hill

Extension: Have students write a paragraph describing Brian's visit to the doctor from the doctor's point of view.

Name: _____ Date: _____

HAVE, BE, DO

> Like most verbs, *be, do,* and *have* change their forms in order to agree with their subjects.

Have you ever wondered what it would be like to be your favorite animal?
Choose an eagle, a lion, a dolphin, a wolf, or any other animal. Write a story
describing your experiences. Use forms of *have, be,* and *do* at least ten times.

_____

_____

_____

_____

_____

_____

_____

_____

_____

_____

_____

_____

_____

_____

_____

_____

_____

_____

_____

_____

Macmillan/McGraw-Hill

USING *HAVE*

Use *has* and *had* to tell about one person, place, thing, or idea. Use *has* for the present. Use *had* for the past.

Marya *has* a cold. Terry *had* one last week.

Use *have* and *had* to tell about more than one person, place, thing, or idea. Use *have* in the present tense. Use *had* in the past tense.

Marya and Terry *have* skates. They *had* warm socks.

Complete each sentence by writing the correct form of the verb *have* on the line. The tense is indicated in parentheses at the end of each sentence.

1. The eagles _____ a huge nest high in the tree. (present)

2. It _____ three chicks in it. (present)

3. We _____ binoculars to spot him. (past)

4. Dad said, "We _____ a good view from above them to see them clearly." (present)

5. The young eagles he remembered _____ ugly feathers. (past)

6. The cliff we wanted to climb _____ easy access. (past)

7. From the top we _____ a terrific view into the nest. (past)

8. Eagles _____ a lot of confidence, so they didn't mind us watching them. (present)

9. The two eagle parents _____ no trouble carrying large amounts of food to the nest. (past)

10. The young chicks _____ no trouble finishing their lunch. (past)

Circle the word that correctly completes each sentence.

11. Walter's new bike (has, have) special hand brakes.

12. I (has, have) no idea what you are going to do next!

13. That cat is running away and (has, have) a mouse in its mouth.

14. When I was born, my parents already (had, has) two children.

15. These potato chips (has, have) a funny taste.

Extension: Have students read a paragraph in their science text and write down all uses of the verb *have*.

Macmillan/McGraw-Hill

USING *BE*

> Use *is* and *was* to tell about one person, place, thing, or idea. Use *is* for the present. Use *was* for the past.
>
> The idea *is* easy. The problem *was* doing it.
>
> Use *are* and *were* to tell about more than one person, place, thing, or idea. Use *are* for the present. Use *were* for the past.
>
> The parks *are* beautiful. We *were* there for a week.

Read each sentence. Circle the form of the verb *be* in parentheses that correctly completes the sentence.

1. John (were, is) Mario's father.

2. John and Mario (are, is) much alike in temperament.

3. Both (is, are) easygoing and slow to anger.

4. But Mario (are, is) sometimes impulsive.

5. His dad (is, are) often unhappy with Mario as a result.

6. They (was, were) going to the shopping mall.

7. But suddenly Mario (were, was) nowhere to be found.

8. John (was, were) beginning to get very annoyed at Mario.

9. When he (was, were) finally able to locate Mario, John reprimanded him sharply.

10. "Next time we (is, are) planning to go somewhere, please stick around," John said.

Write a sentence using the form of *be* given.

11. (is) _____

12. (were) _____

13. (are) _____

14. (was) _____

15. (were) _____

Extension: Have students write a paragraph explaining how they are similar to or different from a parent or sibling.

Macmillan/McGraw-Hill

USING DO

> Use *does* and *did* to tell about one person, place, thing, or idea. Use *does* for the present. Use *did* for the past.
>
> He *does* the dishes. He *did* them already.
>
> Use *do* and *did* to tell about more than one person, place, thing, or idea. Use *do* for the present. Use *did* for the past.
>
> Jeff and James *do* yoga. They *did* the best in the class.

Use the words *does*, *do*, and *did* in a paragraph to describe a time when you were a friend to an animal.

_____

_____

_____

_____

_____

_____

_____

_____

_____

_____

Circle the form of *do* that correctly completes the sentence.

1. The band (did, do) all their greatest hits at last week's concert.

2. "(Do, Does) what you have to do," the captain said sternly.

3. Paul (do, does) the best magic tricks!

4. The Montezes (do, does) favors for us all the time.

5. Lisa and Jeff (does, did) the best on the math test.

Macmillan/McGraw-Hill

Extension: Have students reread their paragraphs and the exercise sentences and write *S* over each singular form of *do*, and *P* over each plural form.

HAVE, BE, DO

Be, do, and have change their forms in order to agree with their subjects.

Read each sentence. Write in each blank the correct form of be, do, and have.

1. Tina's poodle _____ tricks like rolling over and shaking hands.

2. Patrick Ewing _____ the ball now, and he's about to shoot!

3. The first people chosen for the school play yesterday _____ Morgan, Richard, and Carmen.

4. If you _____ the first problem, it will give you a clue about solving the second one.

5. Jose's parents _____ lots to do, but they plan to come to the concert anyway.

6. Mother asked if Marcie _____ all of her chores before she turned on the TV.

7. Ripe, juicy peaches _____ my very favorite fruit.

8. Panthers and Eagles _____ the most popular names in last week's vote for a school mascot.

9. "Ramona _____ the party decorations," explained Ms. Butler.

10. Mom and Dad _____ a good time at the picnic.

Write sentences about wild animals using the verbs in parentheses.

11. (are) _____

12. (have) _____

13. (did) _____

14. (has) _____

15. (was) _____

Extension: Have students read a newspaper or magazine article and underline each use of be, do, and have.

Level 11/Unit 3

15

Macmillan/McGraw-Hill

MAIN AND HELPING VERBS

Write a paragraph describing a favorite older relative in your family. Tell what you like about an aunt, uncle, grandparent, or other older family member.

_____

_____

_____

_____

_____

_____

_____

_____

_____

_____

_____

_____

_____

_____

_____

_____

_____

_____

_____

_____

_____

_____

Macmillan/McGraw-Hill

Extension: Have students reread their paragraphs and underline the main verbs and circle the helping verbs.

WHAT IS A MAIN VERB?

> The **main verb** tells what the subject does or did.
>
> Jason is *playing* soccer.

Read each sentence. Underline each main verb.

1. Johanna will spend part of her vacation with Aunt Ingrid.

2. She and her cousins will ride horses.

3. Aunt Ingrid had given them each a horse to care for.

4. Johanna had hoped for a black mare.

5. Eric and John were wishing for pintos.

6. Uncle Pete was driving his matched team of Belgians.

7. "You will probably fall off the first time, Eric."

8. "You should talk, Johanna!"

9. They could ride in the Independence Day parade.

10. Aunt Ingrid was impressed by Johanna's good horsemanship.

Use each main verb in a sentence with a helping verb.

11. eat _____

12. choose _____

13. decide _____

14. make _____

15. fold _____

Extension: Have students work in pairs. Ask each pair to choose a paragraph
from a magazine or book. Then each student writes out all the main verbs and
helping verbs she or he can find in it. When they finish, they should compare
their verb lists and discuss any differences.

62

Level 11/Unit 4

15

Macmillan/McGraw-Hill

WHAT IS A HELPING VERB?

> A **helping verb** helps the main verb show an action. Common helping verbs are *am, is, are, was, were, will, has, have, had, shall, can,* and *could.*

Read each sentence. Circle each helping verb.

1. Johanna is helping Aunt Ingrid with barn chores.

2. They have mucked out the stalls.

3. Eric was polishing his saddle.

4. She had already washed some blankets.

5. "I am sweeping out the whole barn, Aunt Ingrid."

6. They are using straw on the floors.

7. Aunt Ingrid has hosed down the cobblestones.

8. Next, Eric and John can fix lunch.

9. All of them were feeling very hungry.

10. Aunt Ingrid, Johanna, Eric, and John are sitting down at the table.

Complete each sentence using a main verb and a helping verb that agree with the subject.

11. Spiders _____.

12. The horses _____.

13. Johanna _____.

14. The strong wind _____.

15. The hay in the loft _____.

Macmillan/McGraw-Hill

15 Level 11/Unit 4

Extension: Have students listen to a news broadcast and write down all the helping verbs they hear in one minute.

63

PRACTICE WITH MAIN AND HELPING VERBS

> The **main verb** tells what the subject does or did. A **helping verb** helps the main verb show an action. Common helping verbs are *am, is, are, was, were, will, has, have, had, shall, can,* and *could.*

Write fifteen sentences about some of the things you and your family need to do
to keep your home tidy. Use a helping verb and a main verb in each sentence.

1. _____
2. _____
3. _____
4. _____
5. _____
6. _____
7. _____
8. _____
9. _____
10. _____
11. _____
12. _____
13. _____
14. _____
15. _____

64

Extension: Have students reread the sentences they have written, underlining the
main verbs and circling the helping verbs.

Level 11/Unit 4   15

Macmillan/McGraw-Hill

MAIN AND HELPING VERBS

The **main verb** tells what the subject does or did. A **helping verb** helps the main verb show an action. Common helping verbs are *am, is, are, was, were, will, has, have,* and *had.*

Read the paragraphs. Correct errors with main and helping verbs.

Johanna and Aunt Ingrid was planning to take the horses to the fair. They were loaded up the truck. Suddenly, an old beat-up pickup truck appeared. "The veterinarian coming," said Aunt Ingrid.

Johanna was think that the truck's horn sounded like the honking of a goose! "I wanted to see you," Aunt Ingrid told the veterinarian. "We am running short on antibiotics."

He will never visiting our house in the city, thought Johanna. Veterinarians don't seen many horses in the city. Her family was taken their dogs to the clinic many times.

He jumping out of his truck when Johanna led her mare out of the barn. Johanna was very glad he have come before they left for the fair.

Extension: Have students work in pairs. One student names a subject and the other writes a sentence about it containing a helping verb and a main verb.

Macmillan/McGraw-Hill

LINKING VERBS

Sam's teacher suggested that he keep a diary. Have you ever kept a diary? In the space below, write an entry for a recent day in your life. Describe what you did, the people you saw, the weather, or anything else you would like to remember about the day. Use linking verbs in your diary entry.

_____

_____

_____

_____

_____

_____

_____

_____

_____

_____

_____

_____

_____

_____

_____

_____

_____

_____

_____

_____

_____

_____

_____

_____

_____

Extension: Have students underline each linking verb in their diary entries.

Macmillan/McGraw-Hill

BE IN THE PRESENT

A **linking verb** connects the subject of a sentence with a noun or adjective in the predicate. The most common linking verbs are forms of *be: am, is, are, will be, was,* and *were.*

Pam **is** a *player*. (noun) Pam **is** *happy*. (adjective)

Read each sentence. Circle the linking verb that correctly completes the sentence.

1. Dan's story for the contest (are, is) a description of a trip with his mother.

2. Dan's mom (is, am) a book salesperson.

3. Dan's mother (is, am) very ambitious.

4. The boy's parents (is, are) divorced.

5. Leonard Whalen, the famous author, (am, is) fond of Dan's story.

Write the word in each sentence above that is linked to the subject by the linking verb.

6. _____

7. _____

8. _____

9. _____

10. _____

Now write a sentence of your own using each linking verb you circled.

11. _____

12. _____

13. _____

14. _____

15. _____

Extension: Have students choose a paragraph in a favorite book and copy each sentence that contains a linking verb.

Macmillan/McGraw-Hill

BE IN THE PAST AND FUTURE

Use the linking verb forms *was* and *were* in the past tense. Use the form *will be* in the future tense.

Write the form of *be* that correctly completes each sentence. Then underline the word that is linked to the subject.

1. This lunchbox alarm _____ a big surprise if anyone opens it!

2. I _____ angry that someone took my lunch.

3. Someone told me yesterday that the thief _____ a person in my class.

4. My friend and I _____ really proud if it works.

5. We _____ the inventors of the world's first lunchbox alarm!

What do your parents do during a typical day? Write a paragraph about how one of your parents spends the day, either at work or at home. Use at least five linking verbs in the past and future forms in your paragraph.

_____

_____

_____

_____

_____

_____

_____

_____

_____

_____

_____

_____

_____

68   **Extension:** Have students exchange paragraphs and underline each linking verb.

Level 11/Unit 4   /15

Macmillan/McGraw-Hill

OTHER LINKING VERBS: *SEEM, APPEAR, LOOK, TASTE, FEEL*

Other linking verbs are *seem, appear, look, taste,* and *feel*. These verbs also link the subject with a noun or adjective in the predicate.

> Graham **seems tired.** (adjective)   Ben **appears** the likely **winner.** (noun)

Read each sentence. Underline each linking verb. Circle the word it links to the subject. If the sentence does not contain a linking verb, write *N* in the blank.

_____ **1.** Dad seemed lonely when I talked to him on the phone last night.

_____ **2.** He called just to say hello.

_____ **3.** The grapes tasted great after our long hike.

_____ **4.** I want to help with the decorations.

_____ **5.** Shaun appears calm after winning the spelling contest.

_____ **6.** Put the paper in that bin.

_____ **7.** The water in the pool feels cold.

_____ **8.** The moon shone over the mountainside.

_____ **9.** The brothers caught twelve fish.

_____ **10.** The situation looks dark for our team.

Write a sentence using the correct form of each linking verb in the list.

seem   appear   look   taste   feel

11. _____

12. _____

13. _____

14. _____

15. _____

Macmillan/McGraw-Hill

LINKING VERBS

> **Linking verbs** link the subject with a noun or adjective in the predicate. The most common linking verbs are forms of *be: am, is, are, will be, was,* and *were.* Other linking verbs are *seem, appear, look, taste,* and *feel.*

What would you say to your favorite author? Write a draft of a letter to your favorite author. Use at least 10 linking verbs in your letter.

_____

_____

_____

_____

_____

_____

_____

_____

_____

_____

_____

_____

_____

_____

_____

_____

_____

_____

_____

_____

_____

_____

Extension: Have students exchange letters and write a return note as if they were the author answering the letter.

Level 11/Unit 4   10

Macmillan/McGraw-Hill

IRREGULAR VERBS

Write a paragraph describing a time when you had an idea for an invention.
What did you want it to do? Did you try to build it? Was it a success?

_____

_____

_____

_____

_____

_____

_____

_____

_____

_____

_____

_____

_____

_____

_____

_____

_____

_____

_____

_____

Macmillan/McGraw-Hill

IRREGULAR VERBS USING HAVE, HAS, AND HAD: PAST TENSE

> Most verbs form their past tense by adding *-ed*. Irregular verbs do not add *-ed* to form the past tense. They often have special spellings.
>
> He has *found* the error.

Read each sentence. Write the word that correctly completes the sentence on the line.

1. There are several well-known stories in which a mouse has (told, telled) an amazing

   tale. _____

2. Authors have (delight, delighted) in making us believe that rodents can talk.

   _____

3. Do you remember Beatrix Potter's story in which Mrs. Tiggy Winkle has (iron, ironed)

   all the clothes? _____

4. Writers have (proven, prove) to have vivid imaginations.

   _____

5. Beatrix Potter's manuscripts have been carefully (preserve, preserved).

   _____

6. It's amazing that she (create, created) so many stories in so short a time.

   _____

7. Some popular writers have (drew, drawn) illustrations for their own books.

   _____

8. Winnie-the-Pooh stories also have (give, given) pleasure to millions of readers.

   _____

9. Animal books have (won, winned) many prizes over the years.

   _____

10. How many books have you (read, readed)? _____

Extension: Have students look through a magazine or newspaper article and circle each irregular verb used with *have, has,* or *had.*

Macmillan/McGraw-Hill

IRREGULAR VERBS (1): PAST TENSE

Most verbs form their past tense by adding *-ed*. Irregular verbs do not add *-ed* to form the past tense. They form the past tense in a variety of ways.

Ben Franklin is famous for flying a kite and discovering the electricity in lightning. Use at least ten of the following words in their past-tense forms to write a description of Ben flying the kite in a storm.

fly   ride   run   take   do   see   give   come   go   say   speak   know   wear

_____

_____

_____

_____

_____

_____

_____

_____

_____

_____

_____

_____

_____

_____

_____

_____

_____

_____

_____

_____

_____

Macmillan/McGraw-Hill

Extension: Have students exchange paragraphs and underline all the irregular verbs used in the past tense.

IRREGULAR VERBS (2): PAST TENSE

Most verbs form their past tense by adding *-ed*. Irregular verbs do not add *-ed* to form the past tense. They form the past tense in a variety of ways.

Write a sentence using a past-tense form of the irregular verb in parentheses.

1. (eat) _____

_____

2. (bring) _____

_____

3. (draw) _____

_____

4. (come) _____

_____

5. (take) _____

_____

6. (become) _____

_____

7. (buy) _____

_____

8. (give) _____

_____

9. (feel) _____

_____

10. (think) _____

_____

74

Extension: Have students write a paragraph about what a mouse might see walking around a city in winter.

Level 11/Unit 4   10

Macmillan/McGraw-Hill

IRREGULAR VERBS

Most verbs form their past tense by adding *-ed*. Irregular verbs do not add *-ed* to form the past tense. They form the past tense in a variety of ways.

Write a letter to a friend. Use your own words to describe what happens in a book you have just read. Describe the characters. Use past-tense forms of at least ten of the irregular verbs on the list.

run	bring	make	begin	grow	do	take	write	say
choose	eat	come	give	go	see	ride	build	

_____

_____

_____

_____

_____

_____

_____

_____

_____

_____

_____

_____

_____

_____

_____

_____

_____

Macmillan/McGraw-Hill

10   Level 11/Unit 4   **Extension:** *Have students reread their letters and underline each irregular verb.*   **75**

VERB CONTRACTIONS

Write a paragraph imagining what you would see during a walk on the beach.
Choose a beach you know or one you have read about or seen in photographs
or movies. Use contractions in your paragraph.

_____

_____

_____

_____

_____

_____

_____

_____

_____

_____

_____

_____

_____

_____

_____

_____

_____

_____

_____

_____

Macmillan/McGraw-Hill

Extension: Have students underline each contraction in their paragraphs and
write out the two words that are combined to make the contraction.

WHAT IS A CONTRACTION?

A **contraction** is a shortened and combined form of two words that uses an apostrophe to replace one or more letters.

   isn't (is not)   I've (I have)

Read each sentence. Circle each contraction. On the line, write the two words that were combined to make the contraction.

1. I've been reading a book about people on Hawaii. _____

2. It's an island in the Pacific. _____

3. You couldn't imagine any place more beautiful. _____

4. It isn't anything like where I live. _____

5. We're studying the Hawaiian Islands in social studies.

   _____

6. I haven't been to the Pacific. _____

7. My sister in the navy hasn't been there either. _____

8. But she's traveled to Japan, Australia, and Spain. _____

9. I'd love to visit Hawaii some day. _____

10. I won't be satisfied until I see its beaches for myself!

   _____

Macmillan/McGraw-Hill

Extension: Have students write five sentences using a different contraction in each. Then have them write out the two words that make up each contraction.

CONTRACTIONS

A **contraction** is a shortened and combined form of two words that uses an apostrophe to replace one or more letters. Some contractions are formed by combining a subject pronoun with a verb.

Write a sentence using the contraction of each set of words in parentheses.

1. (he has) _____

_____

2. (I am) _____

_____

3. (we are) _____

_____

4. (you have) _____

_____

5. (they are) _____

_____

6. (we have) _____

_____

7. (you are) _____

_____

8. (I have) _____

_____

9. (they have) _____

_____

10. (she is) _____

_____

Extension: Have students listen to a TV show or news broadcast and make a check on a sheet of paper for every contraction they hear in one minute of listening. Have them write down any contractions that they think are unusual.

Macmillan/McGraw-Hill

CONTRACTIONS WITH *NOT*

A **contraction** is a shortened and combined form of two words that uses an apostrophe to replace one or more letters. Some contractions are formed by combining a verb with the word *not*.

Write the contraction for each set of words.

1. could not _____

2. will not _____

3. is not _____

4. has not _____

5. cannot _____

6. do not _____

7. have not _____

8. would not _____

9. are not _____

10. should not _____

Choose five of the contractions you wrote. Write a sentence using each one.

11. _____

12. _____

13. _____

14. _____

15. _____

Macmillan/McGraw-Hill

15   Level 11/Unit 4

Extension: Have students quiz each other on contractions and the words that comprise them.

79

CONTRACTIONS

A **contraction** is a shortened and combined form of two words that uses an apostrophe to replace one or more letters. Some contractions are formed by combining a subject pronoun with a verb. Some contractions are formed by combining a verb with the word *not.*

You have heard, read, and seen many stories. Write a summary of one that you think you may always remember. Use at least ten contractions in your summary.

_____

_____

_____

_____

_____

_____

_____

_____

_____

_____

_____

_____

_____

_____

_____

_____

_____

_____

_____

_____

Extension: Have students exchange summaries and underline the contractions in them. Have them also write out the words that make up each contraction in the summary.

Macmillan/McGraw-Hill

PRONOUNS

Write a story about life in another time that you have heard someone in your family talk about. It could describe events of a fairly recent time or things that happened long ago. Use pronouns in your story.

_____

_____

_____

_____

_____

_____

_____

_____

_____

_____

_____

_____

_____

_____

_____

_____

_____

_____

_____

_____

_____

_____

Macmillan/McGraw-Hill

Extension: Have students underline all the pronouns in their stories. **81**

WHAT ARE SUBJECT AND OBJECT PRONOUNS?

A **pronoun** is a word that takes the place of one or more nouns.

> Jeremy is going.
> *He* is going.

Use a subject pronoun as the subject of a sentence. **Subject pronouns** are *I, you, he, she, it, we,* and *they.*

> *We* went to the movies.

Use an object pronoun after an action verb and after words such as *for, at, of, in, with,* and *to.*

Object pronouns are *me, you, him, her, it, us,* and *them.*

> Ben went with *us.*

Circle the word in parentheses that correctly completes the sentence.

1. (Them, They) traveled west in covered wagons.

2. (I, Me) think the pioneers had a hard and demanding life.

3. "But (we, us) didn't know any different and were happy," the pioneers often explained.

4. The wagons had shelves built inside, and the women stored blankets and cooking items in (them, they).

5. The family's cow often walked behind the wagon, and the children sometimes rode (she, her).

6. For (I, you) to be comfortable riding a cow, it helped to have a blanket on its back.

7. (I, me) can't imagine riding a lumpy cow!

8. One man usually had a fiddle or a harmonica with (he, him).

9. "If wolves or coyotes scared (we, us)," they said, "we would hide under the wagon."

10. It certainly sounds adventurous to (I, me)!

82

Extension: Have students write *S* above each pronoun they wrote that is a subject pronoun and *O* above each one that is an object pronoun.

Level 11/Unit 5   10

Macmillan/McGraw-Hill

SINGULAR AND PLURAL SUBJECT PRONOUNS

> The **singular subject pronouns** are *I, you, he, she,* and *it.*
>
> The **plural subject pronouns** are *we, you,* and *they.*
>
> Add *-s* to most action verbs in the present when you use the pronouns *he, she,* and *it.*
>
>   She talk*s*.
>
> Do not add *-s* to most action verbs in the present when you use the pronouns *I, we, you,* and *they.*
>
>   I talk.

Write a sentence using the pronoun in parentheses. Then write *S* if the pronoun is singular. Write *P* if it is plural.

1. (he) _____

2. (we) _____

3. (they) _____

4. (I) _____

5. (she) _____

Circle the verb in parentheses that correctly completes the sentence. Then write *S* if the verb you circled is singular or *P* if it is plural.

_____ **6.** They (eat, eats) breakfast at 5 o'clock in the morning.

_____ **7.** She (drive, drives) through Nebraska on her way to Kansas.

_____ **8.** I (like, likes) to read about pioneer families.

_____ **9.** We (sing, sings) tunes like "From Jerusalem to Jericho" and
              "Turkey in the Straw."

_____ **10.** It (take, takes) weeks and weeks to travel in a covered wagon.

10   Level 11/Unit 5

Extension: Have students take turns writing sentences and having a partner
replace all pronouns with appropriate nouns.

83

Macmillan/McGraw-Hill

SINGULAR AND PLURAL OBJECT PRONOUNS

> The singular object pronouns are *me, you, her, him,* and *it.* The plural object pronouns are *us, you,* and *them.*

Circle the word in parentheses that correctly completes the sentence.

1. The wind on the prairie was so strong it whipped (us, we).

2. The walls and woodwork of the new house were so dirty that the family had to scrub (they, them).

3. The beds had real cotton sheets on (they, them).

4. When the girl played her mandolin, the whole family listened to (her, she).

5. Having a friend, someone who likes (me, I), is important.

6. He invited (I, me) to his house for supper.

7. The cookies looked delicious, but Jenny was too bashful to eat any of (them, they).

8. Our class really liked it when the teacher read this book to (we, us).

9. We stared in horror as the tornado raced toward (we, us).

10. Buster the horse was very gentle, and the children could ride (he, him) easily.

Write a sentence using the word in parentheses.

11. (them) _____

12. (her) _____

13. (me) _____

14. (him) _____

15. (us) _____

Extension: Have students write *S* over the nouns and pronouns in the exercises that are singular and *P* over those that are plural.

Macmillan/McGraw-Hill

USING *I* AND *ME*

Use *I* as the subject of a sentence and after a form of the verb *to be.* Always capitalize *I.* Use *me* after words such as *for, at, of, with,* and *to.*

   I saw him.   The guilty one was *I.*

Place *I* last in compound subjects and in compounds following a linking verb.

   Jim and *I* ate it.

Place *me* and *us* last in a compound after an action verb and after words such as *for, at, of, with,* and *to.*

   Dad chose *Sam and me* last.

Write *C* next to each sentence that is correct. If the sentence is incorrect, rewrite it correctly on the line.

_____ **1.** My friend Jon and me decided to read about pioneer families.

_____

_____ **2.** The librarian recommended several books to I.

_____

_____ **3.** One of the things I read about was one-room schoolhouses.

_____

_____ **4.** Jon and I read some of the same books.

_____

_____ **5.** For us, it didn't seem like work at all.

_____

_____ **6.** Me and Jon spent a lot of time looking through the card catalog.

_____

_____ **7.** There was an article in the newspaper about me and Jon.

_____

_____ **8.** My aunt in Cleveland saw me in the newspaper.

_____

Macmillan/McGraw-Hill

Extension: Have students look through a newspaper for uses of *I, me, we,* and *us.*

POSSESSIVE PRONOUNS

Write a paragraph about a trip your family has taken together. Choose a long or a short trip by car, plane, train, boat, or even on foot. Use possessive pronouns in your paragraph.

_____

_____

_____

_____

_____

_____

_____

_____

_____

_____

_____

_____

_____

_____

_____

_____

_____

_____

_____

_____

Extension: Have students underline each possessive pronoun in their paragraphs.

Macmillan/McGraw-Hill

WHAT ARE POSSESSIVE PRONOUNS?

A **possessive pronoun** takes the place of a **possessive noun**. It shows who or what owns something.

Some possessive pronouns are used before nouns: *my, your, his, her, its, our,* and *their.*

 my hat   *her* cat

Some possessive pronouns can stand alone: *mine, yours, his, hers, its, ours,* and *theirs.*

 Where is *yours*?   The game is *theirs.*

Read each pair of sentences. Complete the second one by circling the correct possessive pronoun in parentheses.

1. This book about Canada belongs to me. It's (my, mine).

2. The hopeful people who traveled to North America had hard times. History tells (their, theirs) story.

3. Gold was the reason many people went to the West. (Its, It's) attraction was very strong.

4. Alicia has a gold neck chain. (Her, Hers) grandmother gave it to her.

5. I noticed two gold rings on the dresser. Are they (your, yours)?

6. My cousins are visiting from Alabama. The rings on the dresser are (their, theirs).

7. I saw an old miner's helmet at a museum. (Our, Ours) class was there on a field trip.

8. Dogs in Alaska are still used to pulling sleds. Renata makes (her, hers) pull a skateboard!

9. I would never make a dog pull a person on a skateboard. Besides, (my, mine) dog is a miniature poodle!

10. Bon-Bon is tiny and couldn't pull very much. But Dad says he's worth (his, its) weight in gold.

Macmillan/McGraw-Hill

10 Level 11/Unit 5

Extension: Have students write five pairs of sentences like the ones in the exercise and quiz each other on the possessive pronouns.

87

POSSESSIVE PRONOUNS USED BEFORE NOUNS

Sometimes possessive pronouns are used before nouns: *my, your, his, her, its, our,* and *their.*

Write a sentence using the possessive pronoun in parentheses.

1. (your) _____

2. (my) _____

3. (their) _____

4. (its) _____

5. (her) _____

Fill in the blank with the correct possessive pronoun.

6. When pioneers finally reached California, many ordered fresh fruit and vegetables for

_____ first meal.

7. Many business people set out from California to seek

_____ fortunes in the new lands to the North.

8. Many inexperienced people left _____ homes in the East

to establish farms and businesses in the wild forests of what would become the states

of Washington and Oregon.

9. _____ whole body starts to shiver when I think about the

bone-chilling rivers they had to cross.

10. Can you imagine what _____ life would have been like if

you had lived in those times?

Extension: Have students listen to a favorite song and write down every
possessive pronoun they hear in the lyrics.   Level 11/Unit 5   10

Macmillan/McGraw-Hill

POSSESSIVE PRONOUNS USED ALONE: *MINE, YOURS, HIS, HERS, THEIRS*

Some possessive pronouns can stand alone: *mine, yours, his, hers, its, ours,* and *theirs. His* can be used with and without a noun.

Have you ever been caught in a sudden thunderstorm or snowfall? Have you almost been blown off your feet on a windy day? Have you tried to keep cool when the temperature was over a hundred degrees? Write a paragraph describing a time when you faced the challenge of bad weather. In your paragraph, use five possessive pronouns that stand alone.

_____

_____

_____

_____

_____

_____

_____

_____

_____

_____

_____

_____

_____

_____

_____

_____

_____

_____

Macmillan/McGraw-Hill

Extension: Have students choose a page of a favorite book and write down the possessive pronouns used alone.

SENTENCE COMBINING WITH POSSESSIVE PRONOUNS

You may sometimes have to make revisions involving possessive pronouns when you combine sentences.

Read each pair of sentences and combine them into one sentence. Write the new sentence on the line. Revise the possessive pronouns if necessary.

1. Tom Anderson made his fortune in California. William Volkerson made his fortune there, too.

   _____

2. The mining claim on that side of the creek is his. So is the claim by the pond.

   _____

3. Ms. McNeeley, please put your coat here. Mr. Mancini, you can do the same.

   _____

4. The book on the table is theirs. The one on the stairs is also theirs.

   _____

5. The first report to be presented is mine. The second is yours.

   _____

6. The dog pulling the sled is hers. The one resting by the tree is hers, too.

   _____

7. *Charlotte's Web* is my favorite book. *The Cabin Faced West* is my friend Martin's favorite book.

   _____

   _____

8. Is this shovel yours? Is this pick yours?

   _____

Extension: Have students reread their combined sentences. Have them write *N* above the possessive pronouns of the kind that appear before a noun. Have them write *A* above those that stand alone.

Macmillan/McGraw-Hill

ADJECTIVES

Most science fiction and fantasy stories stretch the truth a little, but that's all right. Write a paragraph, beginning with the sentence given. Tell what kind of adventure happened to you. Use adjectives in your description. And don't worry if you stretch the truth a little bit.

A strange thing happened to me on the way to school this morning.

_____

_____

_____

_____

_____

_____

_____

_____

_____

_____

_____

_____

_____

_____

_____

_____

_____

_____

_____

_____

Macmillan/McGraw-Hill

Extension: Have students underline all the adjectives in their stories.

ADJECTIVES THAT TELL *WHAT KIND*

An **adjective** is a word that describes a noun. Some adjectives tell *what kind*.

the *spotted* dog   a *CD-ROM* program

Underline the adjective in each sentence. Then write on the line the noun that the adjective describes.

1. Digging a tunnel to China sounds like a simple idea. _____

2. All you need is a good shovel. _____

3. Then you need a large bucket to put the dirt in. _____

4. It would have to have tall sides so the dirt wouldn't spill out. _____

5. With all that dirt to haul, you'd probably need a sturdy cart. _____

6. Of course, you'd need a strong horse to pull the cart. _____

7. And a horse that pulls dirt is a hungry horse! _____

8. So don't forget to arrange for a big shipment of hay and oats. _____

9. You'll have to build a wooden fence so the horse won't run away.

   _____

10. Maybe digging a hole to China isn't a great idea after all! _____

Extension: Have students write five sentences, each containing an adjective that tells *what kind*.

Macmillan/McGraw-Hill

ADJECTIVES THAT TELL *HOW MANY*

> An **adjective** is a word that describes a noun. Some adjectives tell *how many*.
>
> We bought *five* pizzas.   Janke ate *several* pieces.

Complete each sentence by writing an adjective that tells *how many.* You may want to use the adjectives in the box.

many	several	few	one	two	three	first
third	numerous	most	all	every	no	second

1. _____ readers enjoy the books of Jules Verne.

2. _____ Verne novels have been made into films.

3. _____ movie that was especially popular was *Journey to the Center of the Earth.*

4. The explorers have a map showing _____ volcanic craters in Iceland.

5. The _____ crater leads the explorers down into the earth.

6. _____ members of the exploring team are curious.

7. While exploring the center of the earth, the explorers have _____ adventures.

8. On _____ occasions, they face great danger.

9. _____ moviegoer can forget the scenes in the subterranean sea.

10. _____ time I see this movie, I get chills of terror!

Extension: Have students work with a partner. Have one write an adjective that tells *how many* and the other write a sentence using that adjective.

Macmillan/McGraw-Hill

Name: _____   Date: _____

**My Adventures at the Center
of the Earth**
GRAMMAR

ARTICLES: *A, AN,* AND *THE*

> The words *a, an,* and *the* are special adjectives called **articles**. Use *a* and *an* with singular nouns. Use *the* with singular nouns that name a particular person, place, thing, or idea, and with all plural nouns.
>
>   *A* boy ate *an* apple. *The* boys saw *the* scary movie.

Some projects don't turn out exactly the way you plan. Write a paragraph about
a plan you've had to earn some money. Did it turn out the way you planned?
Use the articles *a, an,* and *the* in your paragraph.

_____

_____

_____

_____

_____

_____

_____

_____

_____

_____

_____

_____

_____

_____

_____

_____

_____

_____

Extension: Have students exchange paragraphs and underline all the articles in
the paragraph.

10

ADJECTIVES AFTER LINKING VERBS

Sometimes an adjective follows the noun it describes. When an adjective follows the noun it describes, the noun and adjective are connected by a **linking verb.**

Dinosaurs are *huge.*

Underline each adjective that is connected to a noun by a linking verb. Circle each linking verb. Then draw a line from the adjective to the noun it describes.

1. The Museum of Natural History is fascinating.

2. Dinosaurs are interesting to many people.

3. The carnivores, or meat-eaters, are intriguing.

4. Among carnivores, Tyrannosaurus rex is famous.

5. Allosaurus is also well-known.

6. The dinosaur displays at the museum have been popular.

7. Many visitors are impatient to see the exhibits.

8. A trip to the museum next week will be exciting.

9. My friends are jealous.

10. Maybe someday they will be lucky enough to visit the museum.

Macmillan/McGraw-Hill

30 Level 11/Unit 5

Extension: Have students choose a paragraph in a favorite book and underline all the adjectives connected to a noun by a linking verb.

95

COMPARATIVE ADJECTIVES

Think about two members of your family: a parent or grandparent, a brother or sister, an aunt, uncle, or cousin. Members of the same family can be very different in the ways they look, act, and think. Write a paragraph comparing two family members in some way. Use comparative adjectives in your paragraph.

_____

_____

_____

_____

_____

_____

_____

_____

_____

_____

_____

_____

_____

_____

_____

_____

_____

_____

_____

_____

_____

_____

_____

Extension: Have students exchange paragraphs and underline each comparative adjective in the paragraph.

Macmillan/McGraw-Hill

COMPARATIVE ADJECTIVES: *-ER* AND *MORE*

Add *-er* to most adjectives to compare two nouns. With longer adjectives, use *more* to compare two nouns. When an adjective ends in a consonant and *-y,* change the *y* to *i* and add *-er.* When an adjective ends in *-e,* drop the final *e* and add *-er.* When an adjective has one syllable and ends with a single vowel and a final consonant, double the final consonant and add *-er.*

Dogs are *smarter* than cats.   Smart cats are *more* unusual.

pretty, *prettier*   fine, *finer*   slow, *slower*   fat, *fatter*

Read each sentence. Write the correct comparative form of the adjective in parentheses.

1. He couldn't remember ever being on an _____ road. (icy)

2. The road got even _____ when the moon went behind a cloud. (dark)

3. The streets of the city were _____ than he had ever seen. (crowded)

4. He wished the bus's motor made a _____ sound. (smooth)

5. Driving in Washington, D.C., was _____ than they expected. (difficult)

6. It would have been _____ to stay at home. (safe)

7. It was _____ in the tunnel than in the open air. (warm)

8. "I've never felt _____," the boy thought to himself. (lonely)

9. Washington was much _____ than any other city he had ever seen. (big)

10. The first policeman was _____ than the second. (helpful)

Macmillan/McGraw-Hill

Extension: Have students take turns with a partner and write sentences with comparative adjectives. Have one suggest an adjective and the other write the sentence.

SUPERLATIVE ADJECTIVES: *-EST* AND *MOST*

Add *-est* to most adjectives to compare more than two nouns. With longer adjectives, use *most* to compare more than two nouns. When an adjective ends in a consonant and *-y*, change the *y* to *i* and add *-est*. When an adjective ends in *-e*, drop the final *e* and add *-est*. When an adjective has one syllable and a single vowel and a final consonant, double the final consonant and add *-est*.

smallest tree of the three   the *most* awkward of the bunch
pretty, *prettiest*   fine, *finest*   fat, *fattest*

Write a sentence using the *-est* or *most* form of the adjective in parentheses.

1. (friendly) _____

_____

2. (terrible) _____

_____

3. (glad) _____

_____

4. (silly) _____

_____

5. (irritating) _____

_____

6. (greasy) _____

_____

7. (hot) _____

_____

8. (wrinkled) _____

_____

9. (quick) _____

_____

10. (forgetful) _____

_____

Extension: Have students rewrite each sentence to use the *-er* or *more* form of the same adjective.

Level 11/Unit 5   10

Macmillan/McGraw-Hill

PROOFING A PARAGRAPH WITH ADJECTIVES THAT COMPARE

Add *-er* to most adjectives to compare two nouns. With longer adjectives, use *more* to compare two nouns. Add *-est* to most adjectives to compare more than two nouns. With longer adjectives, use *most* to compare three or more nouns. When an adjective ends in a consonant and *-y*, change the *y* to *i* and add *-er* or *-est*. When an adjective ends in *-e*, drop the final *e* and add *-er* or *-est*. When an adjective has one syllable and ends with a single vowel and a final consonant, double the final consonant and add *-er* or *-est*.

Read the paragraph. Cross out each error and write the correct comparative or superlative adjective above it.

Have you heard the songs "We Shall Overcome" and "This Little Light of

Mine"? They're two of the famousest songs of the civil rights movement of the

1960s. Of the two, "We Shall Overcome" is more slower and prayerfuler. Its

melody is one of the most beautifulest of all songs. To many people, it is the

importantest protest song ever written. "This Little Light of Mine" is fastier, more

jazzier, and more joyfuler. "We Shall Overcome" may be popularer, but it's hard

to say which song is more enjoyablest to sing.

Macmillan/McGraw-Hill

10 Level 11/Unit 5

Extension: Have students choose a paragraph in a favorite book and list all the comparative and superlative adjectives on one page.

99

COMPARATIVE ADJECTIVES

Many people don't like winter and prefer other seasons. Which season is your favorite? What do you like about it, and how is it different from the other seasons? Write a paragraph comparing your favorite season to the other three. Use at least ten *-er, more, -est,* and *most* forms of adjectives in your description.

_____

_____

_____

_____

_____

_____

_____

_____

_____

_____

_____

_____

_____

_____

_____

_____

_____

_____

_____

_____

_____

_____

Extension: Have students listen to the words of a favorite song and write down all the comparative and superlative adjectives in the lyrics.

10

Macmillan/McGraw-Hill

ADVERBS

Scientists need to ask questions and find answers every day. So do we. Write a paragraph about a time when you got to the bottom of a puzzling situation. Describe the problem and how you went about solving it. Use adverbs in your paragraph.

_____

_____

_____

_____

_____

_____

_____

_____

_____

_____

_____

_____

_____

_____

_____

_____

_____

_____

_____

Macmillan/McGraw-Hill

Extension: Have students read a newspaper or magazine article and underline all the adverbs in it.

ADVERBS THAT TELL *HOW*

An **adverb** tells more about a verb, an adjective, or another adverb.
An adverb can tell *how* an action takes place.

   The water ran *rapidly*.

Some common adverbs are *quickly, softly, gracefully, hard,* and *fast*. Some adverbs that
describe adjectives and other adverbs are *almost, fairly, quite, slightly, terribly, too, completely,
hardly, really, so,* and *very*.

Read each sentence. Then rewrite each one using an adverb that tells how an
action is done. Use the adverbs listed above or others that you know.

1. The world-famous scientist poured the liquid into the glass. _____

   _____

2. The liquid bubbled and foamed as she poured. _____

   _____

3. She waited. _____

4. The minutes ticked by. _____

5. The clock on the wall struck the hour. _____

   _____

6. In the distance she heard sounds of people coming and going. _____

   _____

7. The foam in the glass died down. _____

   _____

8. The scientist listened to the bubbling. _____

   _____

9. She picked up the glass. _____

10. "My root beer is ready to drink," said the scientist. _____

    _____

Macmillan/McGraw-Hill

ADVERBS THAT TELL *WHERE*

An **adverb** can tell *where* an action takes place.

We found it *inside.*

Examples are *there, here, outside, up, nearby, ahead, around, far, away,* and *everywhere.* Some adverbs that describe adjectives and other adverbs are *almost, fairly, quite, slightly, terribly, too, completely, hardly, really, so,* and *very.*

Read each sentence. Underline each adverb.

1. I thought I heard something creeping around by the window.

2. "There's something there," I said to myself.

3. I crept over to the window.

4. I raised the shade and peeped outside.

5. Looking up, I couldn't believe my eyes!

Use each adverb in a sentence.

6. (quite) _____

_____

7. (almost) _____

_____

8. (away) _____

_____

9. (ahead) _____

_____

10. (here) _____

_____

Macmillan/McGraw-Hill

Extension: Have students write a sentence describing what the narrator in the first exercise saw. Have them include in their sentence an adverb that tells *where.*   **103**

ADVERBS THAT TELL *WHEN*

An **adverb** can tell *when* an action takes place.

   We'll leave *soon*.

Examples are *first, always, next, after, tomorrow, soon, early, today, then,* and *yesterday*. Some adverbs that describe adjectives and other adverbs are *almost, fairly, quite, slightly, terribly, too, completely, hardly, really, so,* and *very*.

Read each sentence. Fill in the blank with an adverb that tells when an action takes place. Use the adverbs listed above or others that you know.

1. Arrive _____ for the science fair.

2. _____ you'll have plenty of time to set up your display.

3. Set up _____ and then look around at the other booths.

4. I _____ make sure I'm on time.

5. I'll see you _____.

Read the paragraph. Underline each of the ten adverbs. Then draw an arrow from the adverb to the word it describes.

    Almost all the booths at this year's science fair were really interesting. First

I looked at one about bees. I found it quite fascinating. Next came a very good

display about hot-air ballooning. It was hard to drag myself from that one. Then I

studied a booth about optical illusions. Soon I was feeling terribly tired. I could

hardly walk to the car!

Extension: Have students describe to a partner something they did last weekend.
Have the listener say *stop* at each adverb the speaker uses. After ten adverbs,
have students switch roles.

104

Level 11/Unit 6

25

ADVERBS

An **adverb** tells more about a verb, an adjective, or another adverb.

Writing clear directions can sometimes be difficult. Using adverbs can be a big help. Imagine an alien has just landed on Earth to learn how to make the famous earthling treat, popcorn. She understands English and knows the name of all the things in an earthling's kitchen, but she doesn't know how to use them. Write step-by-step instructions on how to make popcorn. Use at least five adverbs to help make your instructions clear to a hungry creature from outer space.

_____

_____

_____

_____

_____

_____

_____

_____

_____

_____

_____

_____

_____

_____

Macmillan/McGraw-Hill

Extension: Have students exchange instructions. Have them underline each adverb and draw an arrow to the word it tells more about. Above the word the adverb describes, have them write *V* if it is a verb, *Adj* for an adjective, and *Adv* for another adverb.

COMPARATIVE ADVERBS

Dinosaurs were very different from the animals that walk the earth or swim the seas today. Write a paragraph comparing a large meat-eating dinosaur to an animal that is alive today. Think about where they live, how they move and get their food, and how they spend their time. Use comparative adverbs in your paragraph.

_____

_____

_____

_____

_____

_____

_____

_____

_____

_____

_____

_____

_____

_____

_____

_____

_____

_____

_____

_____

_____

_____

Extension: Have students exchange paragraphs and underline each comparative adverb.

Macmillan/McGraw-Hill

ADVERBS THAT COMPARE *HOW*

> Add *-er* or use *more* to compare two actions.
>
> She runs *faster* than Bonnie. Bonnie runs *more easily*.
>
> Add *-est* or use *most* to compare more than two actions.
>
> Tad ran the *fastest*. He moved the *most* gracefully of anyone in the group.

Read each sentence. Write the correct comparative form of the adverb in parentheses.

1. Dinosaurs walked _____ than scientists once believed. (gracefully)

2. Early researchers thought dinosaurs moved around _____

   _____ than we now know. (clumsily)

3. The dinosaurs that could smell _____ of all were the meat-eaters. (keenly)

4. In general, plant-eaters moved _____ than the hunters. (slowly)

5. The dinosaur that hunted _____ of all was the tyrannosaur. (fiercely)

Using the adverbs in parentheses, write five sentences about dinosaurs.

6. (more slowly) _____

   _____

7. (most rapidly) _____

   _____

8. (fastest) _____

   _____

9. (louder) _____

   _____

10. (more quickly) _____

   _____

Macmillan/McGraw-Hill

Extension: Have students scan a page of their social studies book and write down all the comparative and superlative adverbs they see.

ADVERBS THAT COMPARE *WHERE*

Add *-er* or use *more* to compare two actions.

The river runs *deeper* here. It runs *more swiftly* downstream.

Add *-est* or use *most* to compare more than two actions.

Canoes travel *smoothest* above the falls. I paddle *most comfortably*.

Complete each sentence by writing the *-er* (or *more*) or *-est* (or *most*) form of an adverb that compares *where*. Choose from among these adverbs: *near, far, closely, high, low, deep, widely.*

1. This dinosaur could run _____ than that one.

2. The allosaurus is hunting _____ to the lagoon than the other meat-eaters.

3. Plesiosaurs could swim the _____ of any sea dinosaurs.

4. Apatosaurus had a long neck and could reach _____ than most dinosaurs.

5. Which dinosaur could dive the _____ of all?

6. The baby stegosaurus is following its mother _____ than any other of the animals.

7. The ankylodon wandered _____ into the canyon.

8. Pterodactyl traveled _____ than most other dinosaurs because it could fly.

9. The dinosaur plunged _____ than the others into the murky sea.

10. The diplodocus reached the _____ of all into the cavern.

108

Extension: Have students rewrite each sentence using the *-er* (or *more*) or the *-est* (or *most*) form of the same adverb.

Level 11/Unit 6

10

Macmillan/McGraw-Hill

ADVERBS THAT COMPARE *WHEN*

> Add -*er* or use *more* to compare two actions.
>
>   They came *later* than you did.
>
> Add -*est* or use *most* to compare more than two actions.
>
>   His birthday present arrived the *latest* of all.

Rewrite each sentence, correcting errors in adverbs that compare *when*.

1. Marcie finished the book on dinosaurs more earlier than Rachel.

_____

2. She handed in her report on triceratops soon than I did.

_____

3. The sooner we can get our dinosaur reports back is next Friday.

_____

4. Dontay arrived for the library talk about dinosaurs most earlier of all.

_____

5. Ryan left the later, but he was one of the first to arrive.

_____

Write a sentence using each phrase. Then draw an arrow from each comparative adverb to the word it describes.

6. slightly later _____

7. much earlier _____

8. much sooner _____

9. slightly earlier _____

10. much later _____

Macmillan/McGraw-Hill

Extension: Have students work with a partner to make a list of adverbs that could be used to describe dinosaurs. Then have them write comparative and superlative forms of the adverbs.

COMPARATIVE ADVERBS

> Add -*er* or use *more* to compare two actions. Add -*est* or use *most* to compare more than two actions.

Dinosaurs were amazingly different. Some were as small as hens, while others were bigger than houses. Some ran like the wind, while others plodded along. Write a paragraph comparing and contrasting two of your favorite dinosaurs. Describe their actions and use at least five comparative adverbs in your paragraph.

_____

_____

_____

_____

_____

_____

_____

_____

_____

_____

_____

_____

_____

_____

_____

_____

_____

_____

_____

Macmillan/McGraw-Hill

DOUBLE NEGATIVES

What if you were shrunk by a shrinking machine and were only six inches tall?
Write a list of do's and don'ts that you would have to follow to live in your home.
Think about dangers like pets, kitchen appliances, and doors and windows. Use
negatives, words like *no* and *never*, in your list.

_____

_____

_____

_____

_____

_____

_____

_____

_____

_____

_____

_____

_____

_____

_____

_____

_____

_____

_____

_____

Macmillan/McGraw-Hill

Extension: Have students underline each negative in their list.   **111**

COMMON NEGATIVES: *NO, NONE, NOWHERE, NOT, NEVER, NOBODY, NOTHING*

A **negative** is a word that means *no*. Common negatives are *no, none, nowhere, not, never, nobody,* and *nothing.* Use only one negative in a sentence.

Read each sentence. If it is correct, write *C* on the line. If it is not correct, rewrite the sentence correctly.

1. Science was never none of my favorite subjects. _____

   _____

2. I did not nothing but work on our farm. _____

   _____

3. I just did not see no good in learning about it. _____

   _____

4. Studying science meant nothing to me. _____

   _____

5. I did not like nothing better than raising animals and growing crops.

   _____

6. No one could never tell me science was important. _____

   _____

7. Then one day, my teacher asked how I knew how to take care of my animals.

   _____

8. I did not say nothing except that I just knew. _____

   _____

9. He asked me if I did not know that farming was a very important science.

   _____

10. Suddenly I understood that farming was not nothing but science in action!

   _____

Extension: Have students choose five of the above sentences and rephrase them in their own words using a different negative to communicate the same meaning.

Level 11/Unit 6   10

Macmillan/McGraw-Hill

COMMON NEGATIVE CONTRACTIONS:
CAN'T, DON'T, WON'T

> A **negative** is a word that means *no*. Common negative contractions are *can't, don't,* and *won't*. Use only one negative in a sentence.

Read each sentence. Circle the two negatives. Then rewrite the sentence in two different ways by changing a negative word to a positive one.

1. I can't think of nothing that is more interesting than science.

_____

_____

_____

2. We don't never have one boring minute when we're studying science.

_____

_____

_____

3. Some people say that girls can't never be good at science.

_____

_____

_____

4. I guess they won't never notice all the women doctors, researchers, and scientists in the world today.

_____

_____

_____

5. There is no one who don't do a better job than my science teacher, Ms. Ramirez!

_____

_____

Macmillan/McGraw-Hill

Extension: Have students write out the words that each negative contraction listed in the teaching box stands for.

COMMON NEGATIVE CONTRACTIONS:
COULDN'T, DOESN'T, WOULDN'T, SHOULDN'T

> A **negative** is a word that means *no*. Common negative contractions are *couldn't, doesn't, wouldn't,* and *shouldn't.* Use only one negative in a sentence.

Rewrite each sentence so that it uses only one negative.

1. Nobody couldn't get into the locked room. _____

_____

2. No one never opened the door for a second. _____

_____

3. If nobody did nothing, what happened to the table? _____

_____

4. It couldn't never disappear by itself. _____

_____

5. A table wouldn't go nowhere unless someone moved it. _____

_____

6. No one shouldn't play tricks like that. _____

_____

7. Doesn't nobody know the answer to this puzzle? _____

_____

8. If nobody doesn't explain this mystery, I don't know what I'll do! _____

_____

9. Couldn't no one just give me a hint? _____

_____

10. If no one doesn't tell me the answer, I'm going to go crazy! _____

_____

114   **Extension:** Have students listen to a favorite song and write down each negative
word they hear.

Level 11/Unit 6   10

Macmillan/McGraw-Hill

DOUBLE NEGATIVES

A **negative** is a word that means *no*. Use only one negative in a sentence.

Science is a kind of puzzle that we try to solve. It's like a riddle in science when we get clues and have to put them together to come up with the right answer. Write five riddles in which you give a clue that can lead the reader to the right answer. Example: "What kind of bow is never tied?" The answer is a rainbow. Use at least one negative in each clue.

_____

_____

_____

_____

_____

_____

_____

_____

_____

_____

_____

_____

_____

_____

_____

_____

_____

_____

_____

_____

Macmillan/McGraw-Hill

PREPOSITIONS

It's easy to imagine things in the dark. Trees can become odd animals, and ordinary noises can sound strange. Write a paragraph describing a time when you were out at night. Maybe it was in the country. Maybe it was in your neighborhood or even your backyard. Use prepositions in your description.

_____

_____

_____

_____

_____

_____

_____

_____

_____

_____

_____

_____

_____

_____

_____

_____

_____

_____

_____

_____

_____

116 **Extension:** Have students exchange paragraphs and underline each preposition.

Level 11/Unit 6

Macmillan/McGraw-Hill

WHAT ARE PREPOSITIONS?

A **preposition** relates a noun or a pronoun to another word in the sentence.

in the house   *near* the table

Some common prepositions are *about, above, across, after, around, at, behind, down, for, from, in, near, of, on, over, to, under,* and *with.*

Read each sentence. Underline each preposition.

1. Venus is often the brightest body in the evening sky.

2. You can sometimes see it around sunset.

3. Often it is just above the horizon.

4. The planet is named for an ancient Roman goddess.

5. Venus was the Roman goddess of love.

Complete each sentence by writing a preposition on the line.

6. Mars gets its name _____ another Roman god.

7. Mars was the Romans' god _____ war.

8. Astronomers linked the planet's red color _____ blood and warfare.

9. The red planet is also seen _____ the night sky.

10. It twinkles red as it moves _____ the sky.

Macmillan/McGraw-Hill

Extension: Have students read a newspaper or magazine article and circle each preposition they find.

PREPOSITIONAL PHRASES

> A **prepositional phrase** begins with a preposition and ends with a noun or pronoun.
>
> *under* the *porch*

Read each sentence. Underline each prepositional phrase. Circle each preposition.

1. The broadcast on the radio electrified the nation.

2. An announcer was reporting an invasion from Mars.

3. Frightened listeners gathered around their radios.

4. The invasion seemed very real to many.

5. Had the listeners forgotten it was the eve of October 31?

Complete each sentence by writing a prepositional phrase on the line.

6. How would you have felt if you had been listening _____?

7. It seemed impossible _____.

8. Had Martians really landed _____?

9. The name _____ was Orson Welles.

10. He later became a famous movie director _____.

Extension: Have students write a radio announcement saying that Martians have invaded Earth. Have them circle each preposition they use.

Level 11/Unit 6

15

Macmillan/McGraw-Hill

OBJECT OF A PREPOSITION

> The **object of a preposition** is the noun or pronoun that follows the preposition.
>
> over the *hill*   across the *street*

Read each sentence. Underline each prepositional phrase. Circle each object of a preposition.

1. Space travel has always been fascinating to many people.

2. Hundreds of science fiction novels have presented the subject.

3. For centuries, space travel was only a dream.

4. Only in 1961 did the dream come true.

5. Yuri Gagarin, a Russian cosmonaut, made the first voyage into space.

Write a sentence using the prepositional phrase.

6. on earth _____

_____

7. from another planet _____

_____

8. through outer space _____

_____

9. with suspicion _____

_____

10. after a landing _____

_____

Macmillan/McGraw-Hill

Extension: Have students listen to a favorite song and write down each prepositional phrase they hear.

PREPOSITIONS

> A **preposition** relates a noun or a pronoun to another word in the sentence. Some common prepositions are *about, above, across, after, around, at, behind, down, for, from, in, near, of, on, over, to, under,* and *with.*
>
> A prepositional phrase begins with a preposition and ends with a noun or pronoun.
>
> The object of a preposition is the noun or pronoun that follows the preposition.

Read the paragraph. Underline each prepositional phrase. Draw an extra line under each preposition. Circle each object of a preposition.

The radio broadcast that frightened so many people took place on October

30, 1938. It was the night before Halloween. The radio play was based on a

novel by English writer H.G. Wells. The producer of the broadcast was Orson

Welles. Welles made announcements during the broadcast that it was only a

play. But many people did not hear them, and a feeling of panic gripped the

country. They believed an invasion of Earth was really taking place. The play,

called *War of the Worlds,* told of gigantic creatures marching across the New

Jersey countryside. The best efforts of the U.S. Army were not enough to stop

the creatures. To many listeners, it seemed as if the world's doom was at hand.

Instead, the broadcast was perhaps the greatest trick or treat of all time!

120 **Extension:** Have students work with a partner, one writing a prepositional phrase
and the other writing a sentence using it.

Level 11/Unit 6 45

Macmillan/McGraw-Hill